PRAISE FOR *THE NEW W*

The wedding industry was in need of an overhaul long before the pandemic, but as 2020's pared-down nuptials made clear, the elaborate, expensive, and painfully orchestrated Big Day is not required for celebrating love. As they make clear in *The New Wedding Book*, Michelle Bilodeau and Karen Cleveland get that big time. A modern-day guide to getting hitched (and doing it your own way), *The New Wedding Book* is crammed with helpful advice on everything from ethical diamonds to engagement photos to why it's totally okay to throw diamonds and engagement photos out the window. The authors understand that everyone has different dreams for their nuptials but also that these dreams can give us more stress than satisfaction. In other words, it's a wedding book that doesn't buy into all the wedding hype. How refreshing!

— Carley Fortune, executive editor, Refinery29 Canada

Planning a wedding can be a nightmare. You've got guest list pressure from relatives and seating arrangement drama, bills piling up from the caterer and photographers to interview, all while contending with expectations that you'll also find the *perfect* venue, *perfect* dress, *perfect* flowers, *perfect* first dance song, et cetera, et cetera, et cetera. Even the most seemingly level-headed couple can get swept up in the wedding industrial complex. Let this book be your armour.

— Robyn Doolittle, *Globe and Mail* reporter and author of *Crazy Town: The Rob Ford Story* and *Had It Coming: What's Fair in the Age of #MeToo?*

In a world where weddings are being reinvented out of necessity, *The New Wedding Book* helps you consider the meaning of the day and how to make it yours. It asks the best questions — practical and philosophical — and also serves as a guide to conflict-free communication with the ones you love. An exhale of a read for anyone planning a wedding after 2020.

— Meredith Goldstein, Love Letters columnist, the *Boston Globe* and author of *Can't Help Myself: Lessons & Confessions from a Modern Advice Columnist*

Think of Karen and Michelle as the friends you bring to your wedding dress try-ons who actually care that your dress is you — but for your whole wedding. They'll give you that nudge you need to ditch that stuffy tradition you never really liked and tell you why it was probably rooted in an outdated sexist custom anyway. A must-read for anyone who doesn't want the cookie cutter all-white Pinterest board, *The New Wedding Book* is here to usher in a new era of brides (and grooms). Think less "I do" and more "you do you!"

— Sara Levine, editor-in-chief, Betches Media

Weddings should be like fingerprints: a bit messy, legally binding, and symbolic proof of who you truly are. This book beautifully captures the nuances and natural bends on the winding road toward happily ever after, forks and all. Because there is no perfect wedding, no perfect marriage, and no perfect union. I love the notion of releasing oneself from these societal pressures and instead celebrating love in all its wild formations.

— Mosha Lundström Halbert, fashion director
and *Vogue* contributor

Relationships are not one-size-fits-all, so why should weddings be? This book outlines the many ways you can make sure that your big day is not another generic pre-scripted event but a dazzling reflection of your unique love.

— Cynthia Loyst, bestselling author of *Find Your Pleasure:*
The Art of Living a More Joyful Life

This book is mandatory reading for every modern woman who wants to actually enjoy her journey to marriage. It's the best time in history to be a woman with ambition — and society's wedding culture has some catching up to do. You are holding a hilarious and heartfelt permission slip and guide to plan your wedding and life on your terms.

— Charreah K. Jackson, coach and author of *Boss Bride:*
The Powerful Woman's Playbook for Love and Success

We're in an age of redefinition, when so many "traditional" institutions are getting a much needed update, and the wedding business is no exception. I've always been cringed out by the "classic" North American wedding standard, but this book takes an industry steeped in capitalist excess, heteronormativity, and conformism and shows skeptics like me that getting married can actually be an accessible, personal, and — *gasp* — romantic process, after all.

— Amanda Montell, author of *Wordslut: A Feminist Guide to Taking Back the English Language* and *Cultish: The Language of Fanaticism*

"Women have rewritten every part of our lives, except how we marry." This line from Michelle Bilodeau and Karen Cleveland's delightfully disruptive new book, *The New Wedding Book: A Guide to Ditching All the Rules*, struck me with the force of a ten-pound bouquet to the forehead. It's just so true. The cultural conditioning implicit in what Bilodeau and Cleveland call the "wedding arms race" is both insidious and infantilizing. Thankfully, the newly engaged now have an excellent guide to navigating the minefield of restrictive, often inherently misogynistic rituals previously filed under "tradition." *The New Wedding Book*'s mission is empowering, and its tone is lively. Most importantly, its advice is practical: once you're all fired up, *TNWB* provides useful tools for how to shrug off the weight of other people's expectations and actually follow your heart. My favourite part of this wonderful, modern, extremely timely book is the personal love stories that are so vivid you can practically taste the spun sugar. Essential reading.

— Laura deCarufel, editor-in-chief, the *Kit*

the new wedding book

the
new

A GUIDE TO
DITCHING
ALL THE
RULES

wedding
book

MICHELLE BILODEAU
& KAREN CLEVELAND

DUNDURN
PRESS

Publisher and acquiring editor: Scott Fraser | Editor: Robyn So
Cover and interior designer: Laura Boyle
Printer: Marquis Book Printing Inc.

Library and Archives Canada Cataloguing in Publication

Title: The new wedding book : a guide to ditching all the rules / Michelle Bilodeau, Karen Cleveland.
Names: Bilodeau, Michelle, author. | Cleveland, Karen, author.
Description: Includes bibliographical references and index.
Identifiers: Canadiana (print) 20200393464 | Canadiana (ebook) 20200393537 | ISBN 9781459747111 (softcover) | ISBN 9781459747128 (PDF) | ISBN 9781459747135 (EPUB)
Subjects: LCSH: Weddings—Planning. | LCSH: Weddings.
Classification: LCC HQ745 .B55 2021 | DDC 395.2/2—dc23

We acknowledge the support of the Canada Council for the Arts and the Ontario Arts Council for our publishing program. We also acknowledge the financial support of the Government of Ontario, through the Ontario Book Publishing Tax Credit and Ontario Creates, and the Government of Canada.

Printed and bound in Canada.

Dundurn Press
1382 Queen Street East
Toronto, Ontario, Canada M4L 1C9
dundurn.com, @dundurnpress 𝕏 f ◎

To Matt and Daniel, the loves of our lives.
And to our beautiful children: May you one day marry
whoever you want, however you want.

Contents

Introduction

"But you're getting married! You HAVE to!"

That empty statement is on the other end of everything from wedding cakes to bachelorette parties, lace veils, engagement photo shoots, and selfie stations. It seems that from the very minute you are betrothed, everyone and their mother (perhaps especially your mother) has opinions about what you should do at your wedding. Heck, even if you just decide to go rogue and forego the old "traditional" engagement route, just wait for the unsolicited feedback to roll in. Couples ruminate on things ("At my wedding, do I have to …?") as if the Wedding Police are going to come and arrest them.

Given the calamity that was 2020, perhaps it's time we put those expectations into perspective. As New York–based reporter Ashley Fetters wrote in "The Pandemic's Long-Lasting Effects on Weddings" in the *Atlantic* in May 2020, "En masse, weddings have been dramatically downsized, postponed, or cancelled. The gauzy, fluttery dress I bought in February to wear to a friend's now-postponed May wedding hangs solemnly in my closet, a delicate question mark suspended in the air."[1] She goes on to lament how the 2020 wedding season was persona non grata, how it gave us our weekends back, and how there was no end in sight for this new normal of smaller, intimate wedding gatherings.

In the same piece, Fetters spoke with Kristen Maxwell Cooper, the editor-in-chief of The Knot. "Maxwell Cooper said she thinks that as soon as people can throw big weddings, they'll be back up and running like the pandemic never happened, because 'there's going to be a greater appreciation for these moments.'" Like Maxwell Cooper, we do agree that people will be craving special moments like celebrating the love between two people; however, we have to respectfully disagree with the sentiment that people will jump back into the idea of a massive white wedding to satiate those needs. Covid-19 and our current political climate have brought a lot of things to a head, and at the end of all this the idea of spending copious amounts of money, time, and effort on one day will probably seem like a waste of resources. Sure, there will be those who want to go big or go home, but we can most certainly bet that the majority of people will take a more thoughtful and intimate approach to their not-so-big day.

To put a very fine point on it, due to the coronavirus there has been a colossal worldwide reckoning of just what is truly important. Thankfully, we saw a lovely and startling number of socially distanced weddings that were pared down, yes, but they maintained romance, class, and a sense of intimacy that made our hearts swell. Just look up former *Teen Vogue* editor Elaine Welteroth's Brooklyn nuptials for a truly magical front-stoop-covered-in-florals, block-party wedding that was incredibly memorable. She grabbed a dress from the back of her closet and did the damn thing.

As Fetters wrote, "Small wedding ceremonies could, in other words, become more common not just for health reasons, but because coziness and intimacy might organically become trendy." It stands to reason that this new collective consciousness will affect how we approach weddings — thank goodness we'll be able to celebrate weddings with our friends and family again, even though weddings likely won't go back to the way they were pre-2020. And that's not necessarily a bad thing!

Truthfully, you actually don't *need* to do anything at all (including getting engaged or married). It seems that, as a society, we approach weddings like there is one way to do it and to stray or make a misstep means disaster.

When we factor in the expenses and the stress, why do we bother to get married? Historically, the answer was simple: It was just part of the script. You got married because that was the de facto expectation, and religion played a huge role. We used to get married in religious ceremonies to mark rites of passage. We had weddings to be married in the eyes of God and for protection. Without a husband, women were vulnerable culturally and financially. A woman couldn't own property or really play a role in the community without being married.

In exchange for this protection and security, they gave their husbands children and domesticity. Until the Equal Credit Opportunity Act passed in the U.S. in 1974 (thanks, feminism), credit card applications for women required a husband to co-sign. For generations of women, marriage was the quickest route to economic stability, expanded financial opportunities, the potential for property ownership, and the best shot at claiming a man's better-paid profession or higher wages.

Of course, today women can buy, borrow, and spend (we're still working on closing that wage gap, though), yet weddings still have a whiff of "You finally made it. Now you are complete" about them.

So why *do* we even bother with weddings? The old reasons for weddings aren't really operative anymore. Knowing that almost half of all marriages end in divorce (yes, still accurate),[2] we can comfortably cohabitate in sin, and we don't need a spouse to provide legal and financial protection, why do we do it?

Because, deep down, we believe in love. We believe in the promise of a forever love. No other institution in the world gets the same respect as marriage. Marriage is at the core of financial planning, taxation, immigration, health care, and social currency. It's hard to talk about these things. It's often out of the realm of discussion to fall in love and fathom that your marriage might be one of the 40 percent that doesn't make it. Perhaps that's why we funnel so much energy toward the wedding. If we can just make it grand enough or perfect enough, it will offer some sort of protection so that the marriage might last.

Maybe it is because so little else is sacred nowadays that we hold a candle for marriage. Everything can seem so hopeless. So much about the world is messed up. We want to celebrate hope and bring people together for something positive, for crying out loud. Weddings are a balm for all that. A happy couple deliriously in love is hope personified. We cling to the ritual of a wedding and many of the worn-out cliches that are inseparable from weddings because it feels good to be an optimist.

What's up with that?

Nothing deadens romance like the feeling that you're disappointing a bunch of people or that you're playing a part that doesn't feel like your true self. How is a person supposed to feel like themself when every message they get about their wedding is what other people think they should do? How can couples get down that aisle in a way that feels authentic, awesome, fun, and true to themselves?

You can. We did. And we're here to tell you that it's going to be great. Better than great. You and your beloved can pull off a wedding that's perfect for you, on the budget you want, without isolating the very people you hope to be swilling champagne with on the big day. But to do so requires keeping your eyes on the prize, learning to hear — but not necessarily abide by feedback — and switching out your wishbone for a backbone.

Because, really, what's the alternative?

We have a friend who, a few days before her wedding, confided that she couldn't wait for it to be over, like it was a budget presentation she had to give at work or a long-put-off dental procedure. The stress of the wedding planning was causing frequent and massive fights with her partner, they were going into a paint-peeling amount of debt, both of their families were completely pissed off, and she was over it. It was wedding fuckery of the highest order. She got sucked into a machine that was making her play a role she didn't want to play. Her wedding was Pinterest pretty to be sure (it ended up in bridal magazines), but her best friends knew that under that French lace veil and airbrushed foundation was one really sad bride. And it broke our hearts.

Our feminist sensibilities also flagged that the roots of seemingly pretty traditions were anything but. While the music and hors d'œuvres have improved over the years, many couples today still participate in the same archaic traditions that people did hundreds of years ago, without understanding what they're about. Women have rewritten every part of our lives, except how we marry. We're still getting hitched in much the same way that generations before us have, albeit with the added modern pressures of having it be Instagram-perfect.

We wrote this book because we too were *this close* to getting caught up in that machine, that tempting white-tulle bridal spin. This is an entire industry devoted to making people, especially women, feel inadequate for not following the guidebook — the guidebook that the bridal industry wrote, unabashedly to serve itself. This book is our attempt at calling for a modernization of weddings that gives couples the latitude to do what feels right for them. When we decided to get married, it felt like the bridal industry was treating us like wedding-lusty airheads on spending sprees. As downtown women living on working girls' salaries, we weren't having it. We were quickly fed up with the ever-increasing significance, over-the-topness, and cost of weddings. And since you picked up this book, you likely are, too.

Many of the people we spoke to for this book appear by first name or anonymously, to ensure they felt safe talking about their weddings, family dynamics, and relationships. To the brides and grooms who opened up to us about your insecurities, your partners, your parents and in-laws, your bodies, and your bank accounts, thank you. They range in age, race, gender identity, sexual orientation, clothing size, income, backgrounds, and location. It was a high honour to conduct these interviews, which frequently included tears: of joy at recounting

PERFECTION DOESN'T EXIST

What we do know is that there is a sneaky, elusive thing called The Perfect Wedding. In a world utterly governed by the ethos of social-media perfection and celebrity culture, couples are in hot pursuit of managing and editing every single aspect of the wedding. The dress/outfit has to be perfect. The flowers have to be perfect. The photos have to look perfect. Frankly, perfect doesn't exist. Let's just repeat that so the people in the back can hear: Perfect doesn't exist. So let it go. Instead, seek meaning or beauty or specialness. And don't forget to:

- Let your sense of self be your guide. Be true blue and you can't go wrong.
- Find weapons-grade compassion and call upon your reserves of kindness and diplomacy.
- Include or create traditions that the two of you find meaning in. Don't include traditions that aren't meaningful to you, or make you feel uncomfortable.
- Think of guests who might face accessibility issues: elders, those with kids, or those travelling a great distance.
- Deal with friction right away. Tiny problems can sprout into huge issues if they go unsolved.

The fact of the matter is that weddings are emotional and cost varying degrees of money. High emotions and money are fertile ground for stress, which is all the more reason to protect your relationship. How you make decisions about your wedding as a couple really will shape how you make decisions in your marriage.

There is a quiet, societal pressure that couples are supposed to be overjoyed at every point of their wedding planning. Sure, tasting cake is better than updating a budget, but not every area of wedding planning (um, or life) is going to be fun, emotional, or even interesting. As you make seemingly countless decisions, you might feel really excited and jazzed about some, and completely aloof or bored by others. That's cool and normal. You're not going to fail at marriage because you don't pore over every detail.

their wedding, of gratitude for having rock-solid partners, and of regret over falling out with family or losing themselves.

We want to openly acknowledge that we're both white, heterosexual, cisgender women. When we are talking about weddings, we are talking about the Western wedding as we know it in both fairy tales and pop culture. In our city, we see weddings that cross faiths, races, and every beautiful colour of the sexual identity rainbow. This is our world. So while we undertook this book as a sort of feminist manifesto on the Western wedding industry, we didn't want any person or couple to feel left out. We also appreciate that for some people reading this, the interfaith, interracial, or non-heterobinary wedding that you want to have might not be so normalized in your world. For some of our readers, it might be hard. It might be bold. It might be illegal. That might be your world. We see you.

Are weddings hard work? They might be, but they don't have to be. The hard work is done now, anyway. You did it. You found them. You snagged that stone-cold fox; spent days, weeks, months getting to know them; fell head-over-heels in love; and now you are putting a ring on them (or not!). You found your other half. You have explored acceptance and compromise with this person, and now you're exploring a big-time commitment. If you're anything like us, you think back to your single days when you'd lament that all the good ones were taken. (We'll continue to talk about how society has programmed us to believe we are not complete without a partner, big eye rolls included, trust us!) Then, POOF! Into your life walks this stunning/brilliant/ hilarious/sweet/caring/whatever-quality-you-most-adore-in-your-partner, and you know that you want to go through it all with them. For fun, think back to all the goosebumps when you'd get ready for a date or when you knew you would see this person. Remember how you'd try on outfit after outfit before you met up or bumped into them. Making sure you were wearing "good underwear." (Or maybe that was that just us?)

These emotions are going to be your North Star as you move from engaged to married. You will be lavished with attention, but also come up against some pressure to do things a certain way. Maybe you've been dreaming about your wedding since you were little. Maybe you never envisioned a wedding at all, but your mother has been designing yours since you were five. Who knows?

We hope that this book serves as a little whisper in your ear, to stay true to who you are as a person, as well as who you are and want to be as a couple, and how to use critical thinking to make decisions that work for you.

We found our way and hope you do, too.

Happily ever after,

Karen and Michelle xo

• •

Real-Life Wedding Stories

New York native Alex Sujong Laughlin met her now-husband, Dana, at a book club in Washington, D.C., about six years ago.

"We had been talking for about a year about getting engaged. I had a lot of discomfort around rings. I wanted a ring because it's beautiful and because I love the idea of literally investing money into something that's a symbol of your relationship becoming more official, but I felt really uncomfortable pretty much as soon as we started looking.... I hated the way most rings looked. I hated that ads followed me everywhere. I hated that there was this obvious super-imbalanced expectation that he was going to spend $10,000 (USD) on a ring and that I wouldn't get anything for him.

"I thought about getting him an engagement ring. He wasn't down with it — he only wanted to wear one ring.

"Then, he wanted to have something special to get on the wedding day. We talked about splitting the cost, but ultimately he really wanted to buy it for me, which I appreciate. We chose one that was not expensive, and it was really important to me [to buy it] from the store where they use recycled metals and stones. It was really important to me to not go with a traditional retailer.

"I had thought that he was going to propose over Christmas in 2018, when we were in California, because that's where his family's from. Then, we went to this restaurant we both really like. We go there every year for our birthdays. We went there for dinner, we went into the photo booth, and he asked me in the photo booth as the pictures were being taken. That was in part because I told him I didn't want there to be people around, I didn't want there to be a photographer. It was a very private moment, but there were photos, which was cool."

1 Engagements
You Said Yes!
(Or You're About To)

POPPING THE QUESTION

Now what? Maybe they asked and you said "yes!" Or maybe you arrived at your engagement together over a coffee or in bed, as a shared decision. Maybe you asked them. It is funny how we assume engaged means a diamond-ring proposal, down on one knee. Au contraire. Being engaged really just means you've decided to get married. Hollywood has done an excellent job of typifying one type of proposal, which you will, of course, recognize (mainly the heterosexual type): handsome man down on one knee holding a diamond solitaire engagement ring of a certain size, while a surprised, teary woman (strangely with perfectly intact makeup) nods through his soulful, moving words. Social media has taken this proposal and normalized it to the degree that we all assume that's how it is done these days, which makes everyone else potentially feel really shitty about their engagement. People are hiring photographers to capture the moment, exclusively for Instagram, in a way that reminds us of having a camera in the delivery room. Do not feel pressure to get engaged in one certain way. However you decide to get betrothed is perfect, because it is *yours.*

It doesn't matter how you got there, but we beseech you to slow down and savour it. There is a magic time when you and your beloved are the only two people who know that you are engaged. Think about that. The moment you tell your family and friends, it is public, no longer a juicy, darling secret between the two of you. Once the cat is out of the bag, you can't get it back in, so don't rush it. What if you are the only two people who know that you're engaged for a day? A weekend? A week? Do things on your own timeline because once you share the news, it is going to spread like wildfire. And while you'll certainly bask in the congratulations and good wishes, it is no longer a secret between you and your partner.

And if we can offer one last piece of advice before you dive into this chapter (we'll offer lots of advice throughout this book, get used to it!), it's this: It's very easy to get so wrapped up in planning the wedding that we forget what's really important: the two of you. Remember to take time to still see your beloved, just the two of you, without wedding talk. Your current relationship and your marriage will be better for it.

Documenting Your Proposal (Or Redoing It for the Camera)

The degree to which a proposal (if there is a proposal at all) is public or private is a very personal thing. That's your business. But the restaging of a proposal? We have some feelings. Dr. Chrys Ingraham, professor and chair of sociology at Purchase College at State University of

ORGANIZE A MEAL FOR BOTH SIDES

If your families haven't met yet, you might want to plan a get-together before the wedding plans really take off. Other wedding books will tell you that, traditionally, the groom's parents would contact the bride's parents right after they hear the great news. We say anything goes. Rather than put the onus on one set of parents to contact the other, why not host something to get them introduced? Since you know your parents best, the two of you can find a setting that will make everyone feel at ease.

New York, feels that the focus on the spectacular engagement performance is just the latest element in the wedding industry arms race.[3] Kirsten, recently wed herself, agrees. "This business of staged proposals is all a bit much. Do you actually care about being in the moment? Or are you doing this to create an impression, a contrived moment of your own version of fairy tale. It's this showing off of the fact that your fiancé went all out for you because he must love you soooo much. It is a way of trying to showcase your own value, 'Look how special I am.'"[4]

Sharing the Good News

Parents are typically the first in line to share in the news, preferably in an intimate setting, and the same applies if you or your partner-to-be have children — little ones should hear the news directly from you, in private. If you and your partner want to be the ones to tell siblings or grandparents yourselves, it is perfectly acceptable to ask parents to stay tight-lipped for a few days, giving you time to personally tell others in your immediate family.

A sage rule is that the closer the relationship to the newly engaged couple, the more intimate the form of communication. If time and distance afford it, telling loved ones that you are engaged ideally happens in person (if not, a gleeful FaceTime, Zoom, or phone call will do). Acquaintances might find out through social media, but the people you are close enough to celebrate your birthday with, for example, should hear in a more special way.

Wait until after your inner circle knows the news to tout your engagement publicly, whether that is updating your relationship status on Facebook or arranging for an engagement announcement in the newspaper. (Back in the day, the bride's parents would do this, but now couples frequently do it for themselves; it's pretty charming and a cinch to do — typically just a form submitted and photo uploaded online, if photos are your thing. Just think, your grandkids will love it and be desperate to know what a newspaper was.)

It seems like now every happy engagement comes with a shiny social-media announcement. Some people are even hiring photographers to capture the moment or re-enacting the proposal for photos. That seems a bit much to us, but you do you. If you're into spreading the news on your favourite online channel, have at it however you see fit. Guys, this is your news to share, when you want to share it. Whether you take a weekend, a week, a month, or if you decide to invite people to a party only to turn it into a wedding (we know a couple who did this), that is your prerogative.

If you decide to forego the internet engagement announcement, you can let those important to you know face-to-face, say the next time you have dinner with your best gals or grab a coffee with your favourite former colleague. But if you just can't hold it in, give those close to you a quick phone call to let them in on your joy before you start posting about it online. These are perhaps the most intimate ways to get the news out there. And, even in today's phone-call-averse society, no one will get mad at you for telling them person-to-person.

Proposing in Pop Culture

Ah, swoon. The patriarchy up to its old tricks. Engagements are more than gestures or occasions. They are beginnings, in every possible sense.

The "down on one knee, he pops the question with a diamond solitaire" engagement might be normalized (who are we kidding … glamourized) in Western culture, but it is a far cry from the way things are done elsewhere. In her book, *The Nordic Theory of Everything*, Anu Partanen dives into the North American quest to land a suitable man. To her and her Finnish friends, the obsession of women on TV (via *Ally McBeal*, *Sex and the City*, and later the bridezillas of reality TV) was hilarious. They assumed that the women must be greatly exaggerated, though after Partanen moved to the U.S., she realized the trope of women devoting their lives to finding the perfect husband was pretty on point. And by perfect husband, the implication was a man who could provide financially.

"In the United States, when a woman sought commitment from a man, there was often an implicit or explicit understanding that what she was looking for was someone who, perhaps even over other qualities, was well paid. The first visible hint of this was the diamond engagement rings worn by American women." Anu Partanen writes that her modestly paid writer/teacher boyfriend (who happens to be American) even got swept up in the engagements-must-mean-diamonds allegory. "He'd been lucky — he'd inherited the ring from his grandmother. With a small diamond flanked by two opals, it was the most beautiful thing I'd ever owned. Truly a token of his love, it made my heart swell." But her feelings for the ring are complicated. "Where I came from, engagement rings were usually nothing more than simple gold bands worn by both the man and the woman, like American wedding rings. Only later, at the wedding itself, might the man give the woman a second ring, perhaps with some stones, though rarely would it contain anything as pricey as a diamond. When I wore my diamond engagement ring from my American fiancé, sometimes I felt embarrassed to be wearing something so expensive in plain sight. But more to the point, I wondered why the symbol of our future matrimony had to be a display of money. And why should it display not my financial power, but his? Rubbing my fingers on the smooth opals and sparkling diamond, I felt like Gollum in *The Lord of the Rings*, both loving and hating this precious thing."[5]

How romantic.

That sort of engagement feels at odds with every step society has made toward equality. For heterosexual couples this dance is old, fusty, and not really about equal partnership, is it? Let us play that back to you: He'll take you someplace spectacular (you don't know it is coming … that's messed up). He'll have already asked for your father's or your family's blessing (because, remember, you're just the recipient of this experience, not an active participant). He'll get down on one knee, you'll both start to cry, then he'll present you with a ring that you'll love while you exclaim YES. Magic, right?

But for a lot of hetero couples, the proposal — as pop culture portrays it and many women have internalized it — doesn't reflect the egalitarian relationships women actually want to be in. Whom we marry is a massive decision. It's not a choice made in a moment. It is made in the way most grown-ass responsible people make monumental life choices: carefully. Instead, proposals are built up to be displays or shows of that decision. Feminism has afforded women the opportunity to challenge and redefine all aspects of our lives. Weddings have been slow to change, but proposals? Those aren't just slow to change. They're stuck. In the vast majority of proposals between heterosexual couples, it's by and large still the man who asks the question, "Will you marry me?" We know of some exceptions (shout-out to our girl Alison, who proposed to her fella), but it is almost novel when a woman proposes to a man. Still, the tacit expectation is that the man will make the grand gesture. He spends (his money) on the ring. He is the active participant, she is the person receiving, being pursued.

Dr. Ellen Lamont, an assistant professor of sociology at Appalachian State University, interviewed 105 people about their proposals.[6] She points to symbolic gendering as a reason why we perform, for lack of a better word, the roles that we do. She argues that a persistent belief in distinct and complementary genders — despite the rise of employed women and the decline of traditional households — prevents the formation of fully egalitarian relationships. Her research explores where and why gender inequality persists in romantic relationships. As women are increasingly better educated, more professionally accomplished, and financially independent, performing our genders continues to keep men and women unequal.

THE TRUE MEANING OF BEING ENGAGED

We tend to think of the time in between the engagement and the wedding as just the lead time to plan the big day, but that's not all it is. Engagements were historically time for the couple to get to know each other better. Remember, families arranged many engagements back in the day and the engaged couple were just meeting. The word *betrothed* comes from the root *troth*, which means "trust." *Fiancé*, derived from Old French and Latin, also means trust. To get engaged was to enter into trust. Think about that when you start to make timelines and deadlines for your own wedding. Your engagement period is there to help you better know your beloved and, to be honest, yourself.

Use the time wisely to talk about what sort of marriage you want to have. Set aside conversations about venues and flowers for a while and talk about the real stuff: What are your finances like as individuals and what will you do when you're married? Do they recycle? What role does religion or faith play in their life? Do you want children? Are you planning to stay put or move across the country? How do you foresee your day-to-day life? Who cooks, cleans, washes up, does laundry? Is there anything you should know about this person that you don't yet know, or that they should know about you? And THEN, after these conversations, it is the right time to discuss the sort of wedding you both envision. Maybe you care more about certain aspects of the day, but your other half will undoubtedly have opinions and ideas.

DIAMONDS ARE A MARKETER'S BEST FRIEND

Did you know that the popularity of the diamond engagement ring actually only dates back to 1938, when jewellers were seeking a way to make diamonds popular again after the Great Depression? The diamond retailers saw that engagement rings were decreasing in popularity amongst the younger generation, so they sought to educate consumers about the four Cs (cut, clarity, carat, and colour) to help draw them back to the thought of an engagement sparkler.

Later, in 1947, the phrase "a diamond is forever" was coined. It sought to sell diamond engagement rings as a sliver of the wealthy life for the middle class. It worked: diamond solitaire rings became the de facto jewellery with which to propose, and the diamond industry soared. Part of its marketing strategy was to visit high schools, to preach — er, we mean *teach* — young women about diamonds. They were also the original influencer marketers, gifting Hollywood starlets rings, photoshoots, and scripts to report their giddy engagement story to the celebrity tabloids of the time.*

According to *The Atlantic*, between 1939 and 1979, De Beers's wholesale diamond sales in the United States increased from $23 million to $2.1 billion (USD). Over those four decades, the company's ad budget soared from $200,000 to $10 million a year (USD). It's no wonder that diamond rings are synonymous with engagements, with more than 80 years of marketing force behind that message.

---

* Carrie McLaren and Jason Torchinsky, *Ad Nauseam: A Survivor's Guide to American Consumer Culture* (New York: Farrar, Straus and Giroux, 2009).

RINGING IN YOUR ENGAGEMENT

Remember one of the early scenes in *Sweet Home Alabama*? Reese Witherspoon's character is led into Tiffany & Co. by her boyfriend. She's blindfolded, and at the magic moment he takes off the blindfold, revealing a small army of jewellers ready for her. He leans in and tells her to "pick one." "Oh my god," she barely manages to say. "Oh my god."

It's pretty much a given that everyone will look directly at your left hand when you announce that you're engaged. Or, some stealth peeps may even notice it without you saying a word about being betrothed. Some of us relish in showing off the new jewellery, while others may feel shy about it. To be honest, whoever said an engagement ring should cost at least two or three months' salary is kind of a dick.

There is increasing popularity in non-traditional engagement rings, and we like it. From Carrie's engagement blue pumps in *Sex and the City* to IRL engagement rings like the simple gold band that Amanda Seyfried said yes to, and even couples' engagement watches. Whether it's a piece of inherited jewellery (family heirlooms are a really wonderful way to buck tradition) or just some spoken words, you do you.

Now that we've established that the diamond solitaire engagement ring is a marketing concoction, if you happened to nab this book before getting engaged, feel free to skip it. Seriously. The pressure to get the diamond can be bananas. If the choice is between a ring or a down payment on a condo, where is your head at?

If you're looking for a diamond ring for a steal, do you want to look down at your hand every day and wonder if the diamond on your finger has been ethically sourced, or did it cost someone in a conflict zone their life? Don't get sucked into making a decision that will haunt you because an industry has recently popularized it.

Many of the world's diamonds are mined from countries facing unfathomable conflicts: Sierra Leone, Botswana, South Africa, the Democratic Republic of the Congo, and Angola. Dubbed "conflict diamonds" (or blood diamonds), they account for between 4 and 15 percent of the world's diamonds, and at least 80 percent of the world's diamonds are mined in areas where there are no human rights concerns.[7] So if you're getting a steal on a diamond, ask yourself whether someone likely paid a high price for it to land on your hand.

Looking for Ethical Diamonds

There *are* responsibly sourced diamonds and they aren't hard to find with a bit of research. If you're investing in a diamond, make sure it is a responsible one. Here's how to tell that the diamond you or your partner is purchasing is conflict-free:

- Does the country you live in follow the Kimberley Process when importing diamonds? Each piece should come with this certification, which proves that each diamond legally entering into the U.S. and over 70 other countries worldwide has been vetted and meets U.N.-sanctioned regulations. The Kimberley Process came about after widespread concern over blood diamonds became mainstream in the 1990s during the Sierra Leone civil war.[8]
- Consider buying a Canadian diamond (the country has come to prominence in recent years for its diamond production). If you still want to support diamond communities in Africa but want to only support ethical miners, it's imperative to ask where the diamonds are from. Kalahari Dream diamonds are a big buzz in the ethical diamond community.
- Recycled diamonds are actually a thing, and a thing of beauty. Consider buying a vintage piece or taking a diamond from a set of old earrings and repurposing them. Bluboho, a Canadian jewellery maker, produces gorgeous rings and other special-occasion pieces using upcycled gold and stones. Both methods are the most sustainable option. And we love sustainability.
- More recently, another sort of diamond has entered the market that isn't mined at all. In fact, they don't even come from the ground. Lab-created diamonds are made by recreating the rare circumstances that produce diamonds in the earth (carbon, and more pressure to

WE'RE WITH THE BAND

When it comes to selecting wedding bands, get ones that you each love and will actually want to wear. They don't need to match or even be the same material. One way to make wedding bands a little shinier and more sentimental: making your own bands at a local goldsmith. And here's some fun wedding trivia for you (we want to balance the patriarchal with some good!): Why do we wear our wedding rings on the fourth finger of our left hands? As noted in *Vanity Fair** in February 2019, Ancient Egyptians believed in the vena amoris, a vein that carried blood from the fourth digit of the left hand directly to the heart. So sweet, right? Medically inaccurate, but sweet.

---

* Julie Miller, "How 20-Year-Old Queen Victoria Forever Changed Wedding Fashion," *Vanity Fair*, April 3, 2018, vanityfair.com/style/2018/04/queen-victoria-royal-wedding.

get pregnant than your in-laws can muster), but in a laboratory. Lab diamonds aren't as rare as their naturally occurring counterparts, but damn it they are exciting. They are environmentally sustainable, fully traceable, and a fraction of the price (in fact, according to a 2019 story in *Forbes*, they can be 40 to 60 percent cheaper).[9] Don't confuse a lab-grown diamond with a fake diamond, either. These are legit stones, just from Mother Science instead of Mother Earth. To the untrained eye, mined stones and lab stones are impossible to tell apart.

ADHERING TO YOUR WANTS WHEN YOU COME FROM A DEVOUT FAMILY

M and M's ceremony was basically a Jewish ceremony in English with no prayers or mention of God, set in a high-WASP golf club. "We never talked about either of us converting, but we did talk about how our faiths would play out with children. Neither of us are religious, so now with a kid, we try to honour traditions and blend our faiths. The reality is, as women, we're often cultural directors at home. It's a balance to ensure both sides are represented. We were able to do that at our wedding and now as parents."

Religion can be a tough subject to broach, because it's super subjective and comes from a place deep inside. But how can you mend broken hearts when your parents or family expect a religious ceremony that you may not want? Lay out your feelings beforehand and have bullet points prepped for when you plan to discuss it with them.

"I would use questions as a way to manage conflict without being combative," recommends Fotini Iconomopoulos,[10] a negotiation and communication expert based in Toronto and the author of *Say Less, Get More: Unconventional Negotiation Techniques to Get What You Want.* "I would be asking your mother something like, 'Why is it so important? What about me getting married in a Catholic church is important for this whole thing?'" Asking the person on the other side of this conversation — in a calm and sincere manner, obviously — if it would change things, and if this is something that is going to matter in 10 to 20 years, may also be a way to help them see how fleeting these feelings may be.

"'What would it change if I didn't get married in a church?' That's starting a conversation as opposed to, 'No, I don't want to,' or 'That doesn't make sense for me,'" suggests Iconomopoulos. "If you can continue asking one question after another … Your mom says, 'Well, I was raised in the Catholic church.' 'How do you think that's going to affect the day? Is it going to be dramatic if I was not in a church versus if I was?'" When asked properly, these questions will prompt their thinking without forcing them to immediately cave to your ideas.

In a *New York Times* piece titled "What Changes in the First Year of Marriage?"[11] American couple Sidrah Atiq and Michael Wiseman, who got married in Chicago in 2015, told author Allie Jones that they compromised when it came to highlighting the traditional values of Atiq's family, while starting their marriage how they wanted to. According to Atiq, when she and her future husband were looking to buy a house, her family were not into the idea of them living together before being technically married. So, to skirt around said tradition they got married during their engagement party, participating in what's known as a nikkah. They were legally married that night, they bought a house, renovated it, and then held a bigger wedding ceremony and celebration in 2016.

THE PERSON WHO ACTUALLY DOES THE MARRYING

In most provinces and states, you can legally get married either through a religious ceremony or a civil ceremony. Each requires a different person to "marry" you and your partner.

Whether it's a rabbi, imam, minister, priest, or a maharishi, any religious leader will be certified to conduct a religious ceremony.

If you're not getting married within a particular religion, or if you choose to forego a religious ceremony, there are civil servants, commissioners, or justices of the peace who can get the job done. Do a quick online search for marriage or wedding officiant in your area, and a list of people who will conduct marriage ceremonies will pop up for you. The province or state that you live in will also have guidelines on their government website to help guide you.

It's best to do this as soon as you have a date chosen. Note that you'll need to budget between $500 (CDN) and $1,000 (CDN) to get thee officially wed.

A few hot tips for picking someone to conduct your wedding ceremony:

- If you're not connected with someone through your faith, or you don't have a referral from a good pal who just got married, you really should interview multiple people. Someone can seem great over the phone, but an in-person interview or even a Zoom call can help establish if there is a genuine rapport.
- Most officiants worth their fee (which you should always ask for up front!) will come prepped with a set of questions for you and your betrothed. They will want to get to know you as much as you want to get to know them, if they are truly good at their job.
- Start with five options and see if one is a natural fit with you and your partner. With luck, you'll find someone who shares the same sort of vibe as you.
- Trust your, and your beloved's, gut. If either of you don't feel totally safe in this person's hands, it's a no-go.
- Ask questions. If you have thoughts on prayers or readings, see where they land with this person. Don't drop something on them the week before the ceremony or even the day of. Mutual respect and honesty will really pay off here.
- Don't be afraid to ask for referrals. You should be able to read some online referrals, and if you want more, always ask the person for the information of recent couples. They may need to check if they can hand out said information, but anyone worth having will have at least one to two couples whom are willing to speak on the record for them.
- Make sure they lay out exactly how the ceremony will run, so you get a feel for what to expect, and if they are open to collaborating to create a ceremony that reflects the two of you.
- Lastly, it's important to think about vows when thinking about your officiant. Whether or not you decide to write your own vows, the person officiating your wedding should know, and they should also know a bit about you, the couple. You can easily help that along by

setting aside a night with your honey, getting two pens, two pads of paper (and possibly two glasses of wine), and, without sharing it with each other, write down how you fell in love, when you knew this was it, what you admire most about them, what makes you a team, and why you want to marry them. If there are poems (get sexy with some Neruda or swoony over some Yeats), song lyrics, or lines from books, share those, too. Pop both of these into an envelope and pass them along to your officiant.

OBTAINING A LICENCE TO WED

Cementing the fact that this whole marriage thing is really about a legal and binding contract (if you want it to be — we know one couple who simply had the ceremony and are living happily ever after as a common-law duo), you and your partner will have to procure a marriage licence. And how do you go about getting this precious piece of paper? Well, that varies from province to province and state to state.

Interestingly enough, Canada has some pretty outré options when it comes to purchasing a licence to wed. In Ontario, you must get a licence within 90 days of your wedding date, there is a fee attached to said licence (it varies by county, but can be anywhere from $75 (CDN), like in Tweed, to $167 (CDN) in Ottawa), and you will need to fill out an application form and bring it in to city hall, the town hall, or a municipal office. Licence applications can be downloaded online or picked up from one of the above places.

Head over to Manitoba or British Columbia and you can nab a licence from the drugstore, a florist, the spa, and even a golf course — we kid you not! In British Columbia, you can grab a marriage licence from a drugstore (think London Drugs), an insurance broker, or a lawyer. The fee is $100 (CDN), and you have to acquire the licence within 90 days of getting married. Manitoba is where things get fun! This is where you can purchase a licence from the aforementioned florist, spa, or golf course, or even a jeweller. So snagging a ring and a licence to wed at the same time is easy peasy.

GET YOUR BEST FRIEND TO OFFICIATE

Toronto-based Max Valiquette, marketing and cultural expert and professional public speaker, has officiated four weddings (and counting) and emceed nearly a dozen. "I think for a lot of people, they don't want to impose by asking someone to speak at their wedding. Fear of public speaking is right up there with fear of dying. I've been in enough wedding parties as a best man, coupled with years of professional speaking and media work, my friends know that it's not a big ask of me." There's a running joke that if anyone in his social circle is getting married, the response is, "Max can officiate the wedding!"

Can anyone just officiate a wedding? Well, sort of. Depending on where you live, your wedding can be made official by just anyone, or it might need to be a member of the clergy, a judge, notary public, justice of the peace, or other public servant. Max is none of those things. The catch is that he does 99 percent of the wedding and at the very last moment an officiant with the legal ability to marry the couple steps in to say a few final words and sign the documents. This hand-off is carefully coordinated. Of course, that 1 percent contribution is important, to make the marriage legal, but the magic is in everything else. "I can lean into a couple's relationship like no officiant can, because I know them deeply as individuals and as a couple. What perspective or life advice can an officiant give to a couple that's known them for an hour? And who wants to hear Corinthians again?" Max adds that he takes a journalistic approach to officiating, meeting the couple for dinner or drinks several times to really find what the theme of their relationship is. And the theme of a wedding is not necessarily getting married.

One wedding Max officiated was for a couple who came together after having, essentially, other lives. They had children from previous relationships and had been together for a decade. For them, the theme was not around a new beginning, but rather what has galvanized them as a family. For another couple, it was about finding their best selves in each other.

The way Max officiates weddings is very much a reflection of who he is as a person. "My fiancée asked me to marry her on Christmas Day in 2019. Our proposal doesn't fit the traditional template. When officiating same-sex weddings — or any wedding, actually — my own experiences inform my approach, as I'm queer. When I had my first serious boyfriend, marriage for same-sex couples simply wasn't an option, so I don't approach marriage or weddings as a given." He brings a wider lens to weddings than the traditional vows we've become accustomed to hearing in Western weddings. Max's views on vows is that they are a crucial way for couples to really bring their whole selves to their wedding. "Weddings lose meaning when they're done out of habit. They are like birthdays. You can't remember the birthday celebrations that are just another dinner with people you see all the time. But you'll remember a birthday party that was a surprise, or one where you went on a trip. Weddings are similar. We're conditioned that weddings are supposed to be the most important day of your life, and when there is that kind of pressure, of course we go to what's easiest and simple, we follow a well-forged path." And that path is laden with the tropes and cliched parts of ceremonies that we've come to expect. He points out that people will agonize over a guest list or families will fall out because so-and-so wasn't fit onto the guest list, and yet, in many instances, couples are quite literally making room for a stranger at the wedding: their officiant.

As you can see, each province has their own quirks, so hop on your computer and do some digging to find out all the steps you need to follow in order to be legally wed.

In the U.S., marriage licences are handled mostly by the county clerk's office. Some offer online applications, and others offer cheaper licence fees if you partake in a premarital course. (We see you, Florida!) In California, couples must actually be living together as spouses when they apply for a licence and they must sign an affidavit to that fact. Does this explain why so many celebs seem to shack up so quickly?

RESOLVING THE WEDDING GIFT DEBATE

Registering ... Or Not

Who doesn't love a gift? But, practically speaking, when we enter a marriage these days (we're getting married later in life, if you haven't heard), we're *usually* fairly set up. The fact that we're shacking up earlier and marrying later is well documented, so the odds are that when a couple moves in together (pre- or post-wedding), there are already two of everything. If you've never lived with your soon-to-be-spouse, or have never lived on your own, for that matter, a registry might be genuinely helpful. But if you're like the majority of the population (the average age of men and women getting married in Canada according to the 2011 census was 31 and 28 respectively, and continuing to rise) and getting married a bit later in life, then you might not need all the extra accoutrements. We remember feeling this hyper-commercial pressure to go on a spending spree for things we didn't need. To go from having two of everything to adding an entire other set of stuff feels extra. And horrible for the planet.

Giving a gift to the newly married couple to help them get a jump-start on their household is an old custom. Back in the day, people might show up to your wedding with cheese, cakes, or things to stock your larder (umm, can we bring back the custom of cheese as a gift?) or maybe even some livestock to round out your homestead. Very thoughtful. Now, most registries are focused around cookware, linens, and some kitchen gadgets. Don't get us wrong, we love kitchen gadgets as much as the next person, but registries have a whiff of the patriarchy, and here's why: In the past 100 or so years since registries caught on, the societal expectation was that the home was the bride's domain. Women registered for things that they'd need for their home, in which their partner lived with them but did little to actually contribute to the home. Typically, that young bride was still living with her parents before she married, and her groom didn't plan on stepping a foot into the kitchen. To register, a bride might venture out with her mother or soon-to-be mother-in-law to pick out a china pattern, some stemware, or a few sets of linens for the dining room. Registries sort of filled a need, albeit a sexist one.

There is still something gendered about registries. Even though societal expectations that the kitchen is the sole domain of women are changing, you wouldn't know it to look at how wedding registries are marketed to couples. Most registries still focus on the proverbial pink things of the house, throwing back to a time when the little lady needed to get her kitchen set up.

Of course, every couple needs a stocked kitchen (in which they *both* cook and wash up, obv.), but couples should think outside of the china patterns. If you and your partner hit the smoothies really hard and your blender is on its last legs, go ahead and register for a blender. But if you happily eat takeout six nights a week and are actually both really excited about renovating your home, register for all the stuff you'll need for that instead. A drill? Why not! Camping equipment? Sure! Wine? HERE. FOR. IT. The point is that your registry should reflect you as a couple, not be a cookie-cutter version of what generations before us registered for.

The Knot, Amazon, and the registry site Zola have, thank goodness, modernized to be more inclusive. For example, rather than searching registries by "bride's name" and "groom's name," they now simply ask you for a name. And terms like *partner* have replaced *bride* and *groom*.

Older relatives and family friends may have a hard time with not seeing a registry (and even when there is one, some people will stray from the registry, as is their prerogative), but if you are categorically opposed to registering, just don't. If you *really* don't need anything, but friends and family keep asking you what you'd like as a gift, plant some seeds with your nearest and dearest that you're saving for a honeymoon or a down payment, or highlight a few things that you have your eyes on. Or, in lieu of gifts, suggest a worthy cause that is important to you and your love. It is a cinch to set up a registry online, whether you are registering for charitable donations, towels, or help for a down payment.

However, even when you express your gifting desires, you may get some pushback. (We all have some stubborn people in our lives, right?) So it may come down to a heartfelt phone call or in-person chat with that extremely pro-registry individual. If you do some research on what you want and present it to them with an ounce of frank kindness, hopefully you can woo them over to your side. If, however, like Michelle's family, there is no swaying on the registry front, note that you can always bring items you don't need back for store credit or cash for something you actually want. Sorry, Aunt Betty, we traded in your coffee maker for a beautiful Hudson's Bay blanket, and it looks incredible on our couch! If you need some help conversing with said achingly unyielding loved one, see Negotiating Like a Boss on pages 163–64 for expert tips on getting your way while using a gentle hand and not ruining any familial or close relationships.

Asking for Cash or Donations

Asking for cash or donations in your name as a wedding gift has become more commonplace post the year 2000. Cash can help foot the honeymoon bill, a house purchase, or a reno, or even help you acquire things your badass independent selves need for living well. But there's no easy way to get around the fact that asking for cash can feel icky. This is a personal conversation that should be had between you and your guests. Some suggest adding this information to your wedding website (we are still unsure of how we feel about wedding websites, tbh), which is one option. Another option is an online cash registry like Zola or Honeyfund.

Enlisting your parents, siblings, and friends to help spread the word can also help. Keep them abreast of your plans before you send out your invitations, as you may have some convincing to do with them as well (but hopefully not). By making sure they're on board, you'll help take away any catty gossiping at your expense.

When it comes to donations, the same applies. Giving to a charity can be extremely personal, so make sure your guests understand why you are foregoing gifts and asking for a donation in your honour. Perhaps even have an anecdote on hand about how said charity has helped a loved one or how the cause is something you vehemently stand behind. Given the state of the world right now, charitable donations can be a pretty easy sell.

Saying "No, Thank You" to Gifts

Asking for no gifts at all is relatively new in the wedding sphere. And we get it. This tradition can feel obligatory, with some even finding it unnecessary. If this is where you and your partner are at, get the word out early through your closest relatives and friends. Some people have added a note like "Your presence is your present" to invitations, but that might not always deter people. This one is so engrained that you may find there will be a lot of defending here. Stand your ground but know that some may go against your wishes. Try to be gracious even in the face of wedding guest disobedience.

Thanking Your People Properly

Thank-you gifts and some heartfelt notes are a given. These people are going the distance for you, so thank them. And properly. No emails or texts. Pen to paper.

You're going to sit down, divide a stack of thank-you cards into two piles, and you and your love are going to write thank yous for every

TRACK NOW FOR EASIER THANKING LATER

As you receive gifts, which might start to happen before the wedding, write down the details of every gift you receive. Add a sheet to your planning spreadsheet or whatever you're using to track your planning. Don't tell yourself that you'll remember later. You will NOT remember later. Do it now, so when it comes time to write thank-you cards, you can specifically reference the gift. It also gives some context for your own future gift giving planning. Let's say one sibling got you a weekend at the spa for your wedding and the other got you a gas station gift card. You know who is getting the better Christmas present next year. Just kidding. (Sort of.) But seriously, it can be helpful to reference what people got you for your wedding when you are shopping for their wedding gift, if trying to be in the same ballpark is your thing.

HOW TO WRITE AMAZING THANK-YOU NOTES

- Communicate your gratitude and explicitly call out the gift or action for which you're writing the thank you note.
- Explain how it made you feel and how much it meant to you.
- End with a forward-thinking thought on how you hope to see or speak to them soon.
- Sign off with the right degree of fuzziness ("Many thanks," "With love," or "Yours truly").

kind gesture, every gift, everything. Make the time to do this before your wedding. If you're keen you can send these out for engagement parties, showers, etc. These are generally smaller affairs and can help prep you for the heavy thank-you card workload post ceremony/party.

CALLING OFF THE WEDDING

Okay, sit down for this part. Not every engagement is going to end with a wedding. Some engagements get called off. Of course, this doesn't tidily fit into the celebratory wedding narrative and so the subject is verboten.

A relationship advice thread on Reddit about people who have called off their engagements showed that many share something in common: a moment that at the time seemed fairly small and insignificant, but planted a seed that they couldn't ignore that something wasn't right.[12] Some engagements were called off because they realized that they were more interested in a wedding than a marriage. Others conceded that they were just in love with the idea of love. Some realized they just weren't ready to make this commitment. It doesn't matter. In the wise words of author Cheryl Strayed (she wrote this in her "Dear Sugar" column for the Rumpus in 2011 and it still tracks!), "You are not a terrible person for wanting to break up with someone you love. You don't need a reason to leave. Wanting to leave is enough."[13]

So, what are garden-variety jitters versus legitimate doubts? Only you know. But if there is a small voice inside you that says "no," listen to it. Because you might be able to silence it for a few more weeks, or even until your kids graduate high school, but it isn't going away. If you know that deep down you're not ready to fully and enthusiastically commit to the person you're slated to marry, pump the breaks now.

If any of this is making you realize something that you've been reluctant to realize, end things sooner rather than later. Don't marry someone if there is a part of your heart that says no. Even if you've put deposits on vendors, told the world you're getting married, do it now. It will only be harder the longer you ignore your gut. Know that this happens sometimes and the price of being true to yourself is more important than losing any deposit.

Heartache aside, cancelling a wedding isn't terribly hard to do. Every contract you've signed already has a provision in it accounting for this. You'd return the engagement ring (don't even @ us — the ring gets returned to the person who gave it to you) and send back gifts to the people who sent them. Mail out cards (or call, or email) to anyone who was invited to the wedding, explaining that the marriage between [name] and [name] will not take place.

As impossible as calling off a wedding might seem, it is easier than a divorce. Sorry to be a buzzkill, but this is a crucial discussion that is often edited out of wedding books and magazines because it is not at all romantic.

AGREEING TO A PRENUP ... OR NOT?

Competing in a close race for the most uncomfortable topics in this book (see previous section on calling off a wedding) is the subject of prenuptial agreements. They are designed to help protect someone's financial position, family property, or one partner from the others partner's debts when going into a marriage, so that if the marriage ends the parties won't lose the assets and income that they brought into the marriage. A prenup can also help in ironing out the details of a divorce, if it comes to that.

They put a very fine point on financial imbalances in a relationship, which, depending on what side of that imbalance a person is on, can prompt some intense feelings. Jeff Rechtshaffen, a Toronto-based lawyer, points out that a basic tenet of family law spells out that "everything you own before marriage is yours and that the wealth you accrued during marriage is to be divided equally between the spouses." According to 2017 data from Ipsos, only 8 percent of Canadians have prenuptial agreements. About 14 percent of married Americans have a prenup, according to a 2016 study from George Mason University in Virginia and Stanford Law School in California.[14] Here's the thing: If you think that a prenup might solve feelings of inequity in your relationship, it could exacerbate feelings of an imbalance. Are you building something together, in *every* possible sense?

William Bradford Wilcox, director of the National Marriage Project at the University of Virginia, wonders why couples concerned with prenups bother marrying at all. In a piece he authored in the *New York Times*, he cautions that if couples are thinking about a prenup or one partner is pushing one on the other, that could be seen as a red flag.[15] He believes if someone is so concerned about protecting their financials that perhaps the couple should just live together instead of becoming legally married. Wilcox also refers to common-law cohabitation, and how in most states those couples are able to walk away from relationships with their money matters separate, and there's no need to spend that money on a divorce. As Wilcox sees it, if you're truly head-over-heels in love, and you're open to sharing a life, children, and finances together, then marriage is a route worth considering. His research supports that taking an other-centred approach to marriage (as opposed to the self-centred approach that a prenup posits), is less likely to lead to divorce and more likely to create a happier marriage. Final point on the subject: Married couples who do not pool their income are 145 percent more likely to end up in divorce court, compared to couples who share a bank account.[16]

• •

Real-Life Wedding Stories

Toronto couple Tessa and Petr married in 2020 at the height of the Covid-19 pandemic and, damn it, managed to still host a gorgeous, romantic wedding.

Tessa explained that neither she nor Petr wanted a big spectacle. "When I first moved to Toronto, I worked in the Distillery District and I worked hundreds of weddings. Most of them were super expensive, most of them were pretty extravagant and over-the-top." What these weddings had in pomp, they lacked in heart. "I didn't feel any actual love in the room. It kinda felt like it was more about everybody else."

When it came to planning their own wedding, they knew what they didn't want: that wedding-factory experience. They contemplated city hall, but their parents weren't into it. "The first thing my Dad said was, 'No, no, no, no, no, no. We need to have something big. We need to have people, we have to have family flown in, we have to do all of these things.'"

It started to stress Tessa and Petr out. "It didn't really align with who we are as people, and we're both artists as well and we're both pretty philanthropic. So it just felt like a huge waste when we knew what our relationship was worth outside of that, you know, kind of like putting economic strain on ourselves just to have a party for one day when we're perfectly happy with nothing at all."

A friend of theirs opens up her art gallery for micro-weddings, with small ceremonies and cocktail parties inside the gallery, all totally turnkey (i.e., a pre-packaged, already-assembled event). She arranges passed food, an open bar, champagne toasts, a photographer, live music, and party favours, all for $3,000 (CDN). "Our friend was like, 'We can do something small.' And we thought, okay, we can split the difference a little and have something so family members can attend, but kind of draw the line at immediate family and very close friends. So yeah, we just compromised. And funnily enough, here we are and we kind of did exactly what we wanted to in the end."

For Petr, the micro-wedding idea was a perfect plan. "We wanted to keep it small, and only invited people we'd want to have over at our house for dinner. We are also expecting a baby in the summer, so April felt comfortable for our timeline." It was indeed a perfect plan, until Covid-19 ruined every plan made in 2020.

Both Tessa and Petr are from immigrant families. Petr's family came to Canada from the Czech Republic, and Tessa's mother's family emigrated from Italy to Argentina and then later to Canada, and her dad's family was originally from Jamaica. "As everything started unfolding with Covid-19 in mid-March, we realized our wedding wasn't going to happen. We were a bit in denial at first. But things got more real every day. Nearly half of our guests were flying in from elsewhere."

On March 20, they made the heart-wrenching decision to call it off. They sent a note to all their guests cancelling the wedding. With a baby on the way, the idea of postponing didn't seem feasible. So what do you do when life hands you lemons? Well, if you're Tessa and Petr, you plan a wedding in two goddamn weeks.

Tessa reminisces about making it happen: "We're in this crisis situation and things are changing so rapidly. Like, just a week before, I had family visit, I was taking my nephew to all sorts of places, and the next week it was unheard of to do something like that." They stripped it down to bare bones, only what is needed to make a wedding happen: "Two people, an officiant, and a space big enough for us to all stand two metres apart was really all that we were looking for in that moment so that we could be married.

"It was actually really beautiful during our ceremony. The officiant said, 'Just look at each other, don't look anywhere else.' And it wasn't even hard to do that because there was really nobody else there, and the whole thing was just us looking into each other and being with each other.

"And I think that's what it's supposed to be about. And we just got to come home and talk about it together after. We could bask in the whole thing together versus most weddings, you're not really with your partner — you can speak to your partner, obviously, you sit beside them during dinner or whatever, and you dance with them maybe. But there's no meaningful digression of events, I guess, until much later. It was nice to just experience that together."

Looking back, the couple agrees that it felt like them. "Honestly the more we think about it, I think it was done exactly right. We got exactly what we wanted with just our two witnesses and our ceremony with just each other, and then we'll get to celebrate getting through all of this together afterward and actually officially celebrate our marriage with everyone."

2 Wedding Planning 101
It's Your Day
(Inspired by YOU!)

Now that your engagement business is done and dusted, you've talked through the perils and perks of a wedding registry, and you're starting to get your head around planning a wedding: you need a plan for your plan. This book will help, but you'll also need to be super organized. Use a notebook, set up a shared document, download a wedding organization app — options abound. Find a system that works for the two of you. Staying organized will help mitigate stress and unforeseen costs.

PLANNING IN FUN, EFFECTIVE, AND SMART WAYS

- Create the mother of all to-do lists, then organize it by when things are due.
- Take screenshots and photos of things so you can easily reference them on your phone. If you were the person with all the highlighters in high school, go the extra mile by setting up different albums to sort them in.
- Add people to your contacts list with all of their details, so you can easily pull up your florist without having to search through all your emails to get their number.
- Keep all your digital stuff in one place (like an email folder, or on Google Drive) and your printed stuff all in one central place. Keep copies of all your contracts and estimates.
- Put key dates and budget notes into your phone, like "Second deposit on venue due Monday, $2,500," so you won't fall behind.

As you start to gather inspiration (and quotes to bring your vision to life), it isn't a bad idea to assume that the two of you will be paying for everything. We go hard on costs and budgeting later in the book, by the way, but as you start to plan, know that the days of the bride's parents paying for the majority of wedding costs are long gone. Plan to pay for everything yourselves and if your families offer to chip in, great. This way, you're not pre-emptively falling in love with anything that you can't afford. According to a recent survey of wedding professionals for the annual International Wedding Trend Report,[17] almost one third (33%) of couples were funding the majority of their own expenses. There are no rules for who pays for what, so make no assumptions. It is better to be pleasantly surprised.

KEEPING YOUR COOL IN THE FACE OF STRESS

Need to tap into a little confidence when it comes to getting your way for your wedding? Ahem, don't we all. Tip number one, remember, it's YOUR wedding. Tip number two, remember that the people you are dealing with — your friends and family — are human beings that you ideally want to keep in your life afterward. Right? The general approach when it comes to having your day your way is to keep your stance firm but open. The golden rule most definitely applies here — treat others how you would want to be treated. That usually includes honesty, compassion, and thoughtfulness.

BTW, when did those three ideals go out the window because someone was planning a wedding? Oh right, when we started idolizing the bridezilla and groomzilla tropes. Elaine Lui, aka LaineyGossip, the powerhouse celebrity columnist and television personality, says, "I think that the publicity around celebrity weddings led to or fed into the rise of the bridezilla, because people were seeing these celebrities have these over-the-top weddings and how amazing it was. And then they wanted the same for themselves and people started focusing so much on the presentation of their wedding."

Can we say no more, please?! Thankfully, being kind is cool again, so let's lean into that as we get this wedding started, shall we? You *can* get through it all without acting like an asshole. In fact, we implore you.

There is nothing cute or funny about a bridezilla/groomzilla. Some people may grate your nerves as stresses run high. Family, friends, and your partner may annoy or frustrate you, but check yourself, too.

As someone about to get married, yes, you will be the centre of attention. That doesn't mean you can start acting like a diva. We'll remind you that no one cares about your wedding as much as you do. What might seem like absolute devastation (the flowers that I want aren't in season and can't be shipped in, *wah, wah, wah*) doesn't *really* matter in the grand scheme of things. If the process of planning a wedding is isolating for your favourite people, or if they feel like they don't know you anymore, then you're probably a bridezilla.

PUT EVERYTHING IN PERSPECTIVE

"I am from a big Pakistani family and my wife grew up as an only child in Toronto. My mother wanted us to have a large traditional wedding. We were set on a small one and fell in love with the perfect venue: an old bookstore in our neighbourhood. We had an intimate wedding for about 65 guests. As an olive branch to my mom (I didn't want her to feel disrespected), my sister suggested that I send my mom and her to the spa for the day. They arrived at the wedding looking fresh faced and so relaxed. And we were relaxed because we didn't have to worry about my mom fretting around the bookstore while we set up."

* * *

"My mother-in-law has offered to book us a videographer for our wedding. (Okay, that's putting it gently: She basically researched and found a videographer and just wants us to say yes to the idea.) I find videographers totally distracting at weddings and, to be honest, a bit tacky.

I talked about it with my partner and he agreed. We figured his mom = conversation for him to have. He told her we're not into the idea but thanked her for her really generous offer. I'd like to say that it went over well, but honestly, she was pissed off. He smoothed it out with her, and I'm grateful that it was him, not me, because he knows her so well. We all eventually moved on and I don't regret the decision at all to pass on a videographer."

Seriously, hear us out. Before your engagement, you were a blast to be around and just loved your friends and family. But now that you're in the throngs of planning a wedding, they are all selfish or insensitive. Sound at all familiar? If so, it isn't them, honey. It is you.

If you find that you only have time to think about and talk about your wedding plans, and nothing else, get a grip.

Don't get us wrong: planning ANY event comes with some stress, though that doesn't give you grounds to act like a jerk. The reality is that every person who is tied up in your wedding has their own stuff going on. While you are working through your plans, they might be dealing with a health scare, a rough patch in their marriage, a crisis at work, or simply dealing with the current shitstorm we call life. Keep that in perspective.

PLANNING FOR YOUR PLAN

Have a big, juicy brainstorm together and talk about weddings that you've been to and had a ball at, incredible spaces that you both love to visit, or trips that have inspired you. Don't think for one hot second about what your friends and family might expect or envision for you. Focus solely on you two lovebirds. The rules of a brainstorm are this: Every single contribution counts, and no idea gets shot down in the moment. Nothing sinks your partner's battleship like criticizing how they envision their wedding the moment they share it with you.

Here are two critical things to think about. First off, landing on the vibe of your wedding is a huge step and it is okay if you don't perfectly agree; resolve just to meet in the middle. We're not talking colour themes here; we're talking about the energy of the day and how it will feel to you and your guests. Elegant? Sophisticated? Charming? Intimate? Spiritual? Relaxed? Rustic? Write it down.

And second: Do you want a massive party with all your family and friends, or a super intimate ceremony and small reception? Try to articulate why you envision this and what appeals to you about it. Give your partner space to articulate their vision, too. Write everything down.

PEOPLE REALLY DO MEAN WELL WHEN GIVING UNSOLICITED ADVICE

Most people have such nostalgia around their own wedding and will freely share advice about how they did things (or plan to do them when they get hitched), hoping you might find these tips helpful. And you might find these suggestions the opposite of helpful. But such suggestions are merely that: helpful suggestions. You cannot please everyone, so best to gently set out your planning parameters. Whether you feel stuck in a gridlock with your mother-in-law over flowers, or you're being snubbed by your sister for choosing cake over the cupcakes she offered to bake, here's how to finesse some well-intentioned suggestions.

Hear them out. Most people chiming in with suggestions genuinely want to help and their ideas are often couched in either how they did things at their wedding, or what they envision for you. They simply want to know that you have heard what they have to say. If your mother-in-law is waxing about how much she loves peonies, ask her to tell you more. What was her bouquet like? How many bridesmaids did she have again? Does she have peonies in her garden?

Acknowledge their suggestions but have conviction in your decision. Clearly let the other person know that you've heard their suggestion — an acknowledgement might be all they are after, and then you can't be faulted for not hearing them out. Tell your mother-in-law the peony bouquet in her wedding photos looked gorgeous, but you really have your heart set on hydrangeas, for example. If you waffle or ask her what she thinks of hydrangeas, you might be inviting more helpful suggestions so be mindful of how the discussion ends.

Carry on. You can make people feel included in your planning without feeling pressure to let others make decisions for you. And while compromise is key between you and your partner, it is not the end of the world if your mother-in-law isn't in love with your floral arrangements. Being rude to her, however, might be. Just remember: The communication lines you establish and the grace you exude will far outlast your wedding day.

Once you have a nice list of vibes that you both like and a general sense of size, you're ready to start thinking about venues that fit within these parameters. Please, we beg you, don't do the opposite and sit down to write a guest list first. It will fuck everything up and you'll then be stuck reverse-engineering plans. Vibe and size come first. Another crucial reason for this order of things is so that when you start chatting with family and friends, you already have a clear north star. Deciding on your vibe and size should be non-negotiable. There will be plenty of room for negotiating later, but agree to not waver from these two things. When your helpful in-laws suggest the glitzy hotel downtown, you can together say, "You know, we landed on having an intimate little wedding with a really sweet, charming vibe and found the most beautiful art gallery we're going to visit next week. Here, we can show you some photos of it!"

While you're scoping out venues, you might also want to start looking for some inspiration. Yes, there are some great ideas on Pinterest or in bridal magazines, but cast a wider net. Flip through some design and decor magazines, visit some different restaurants and stores together.

TAKE NOTES TO GET TO KNOW YOUR IN-LAWS

You might be in the early stages of getting to know your new in-laws or might not know them at all. There might be a lot of new names and faces to remember, along with details of who is married to who and which children belong to which parents. Pop a note into your phone with these details. As you meet people, you can make a little cheat sheet about each person, how to pronounce their name, or little things that will help avoid an awkward moment in the future.

Don't overlook a space because you've been to other weddings there. If you love a venue, you can put your stamp on it.

Put yourself on a restricted diet of only a tiny bit of wedding content. It is so easy to fall down the rabbit hole. Wedding stress is contagious. If you couldn't care less about the sort of chairs at your reception, and end up reading 12 articles, scroll endlessly on Pinterest, and pore over forums on the pros and cons of different chairs, trust us: you'll suddenly start sweating the chairs at your wedding.*†

CONSTRUCTING A BRIDE

There's a lot of cultural conditioning to unpack around how women are groomed to be brides. Getting married is often seen as the finale to most stories with happy endings, and from fairy tales to rom-coms to Disney movies, the message has historically been that a woman's

---

* And who wants to be stressing about, of all things, chairs?

† No offence intended to readers who are deeply concerned about their chair situation on their wedding.

worth is tied up in her ability to snag a husband. We're *supposed* to want a wedding. We're *supposed* to imagine our wedding. We're *supposed* to craft a narrative about the sort of bride we want to be and the sort of wedding we want to have. Men? Less so. There's no stack of overpriced groom magazines. There isn't *Say Yes to the Suit*. Last time we checked, weddings are synonymous with brides, and grooms are sort of on the periphery.

Reframing Your Big Day

The tacit pressure on brides to feel like a princess or celebrity for one day requires a boatload of cash. Did brides of non-royal origin always roll up in fancy cars? No. Did couples always have engagement parties, showers, bachelorettes, and bachelor parties? No. Did proposals always involve a diamond solitaire ring? Nope. But wedding dresses were always white, right? Wrong again. All of these things that we take for granted as being "traditional" are relatively new constructs. There's nothing really traditional about them at all.

We need look no further than pop culture as the root of our messed-up obsession with weddings over a good, strong marriage. We practically salivate over celebrity engagements, meticulously picking apart their bridal look. We were raised on and continue to watch bad television (ahem, *Who Wants to Marry a Millionaire*, *Race to the Altar*, *Say I Do*, *The Bachelor*, *The Bachelorette*, *Marry Me Now*, *Married at First Sight*, *Love Is Blind*) that fuels this narrative. We couldn't care less how many of these fungible couples last or how many times they marry and remarry. We only care about the weddings. We have endless evidence around us that however "perfect" a wedding may look, it has nothing to do with the couples' chances of actually staying married.

We exist in a culture that is obsessed with perfect weddings but doesn't seem to have much time for striving for perfect marriages. Makeup artist Bobbi Brown, when featured on an episode of *Martha Stewart Living*, enthused that your wedding is "your one day to be on stage, to be the centre of attention." There's more left unsaid, too. That

AVOIDING MISCOMMUNICATION

The hype of planning a wedding might offer a nice distraction from some stuff you need to work on in your relationship, but no one can hide behind wedding planning forever. You can hide on Pinterest looking for floral inspiration all you like, but if you and your partner are arguing constantly over how much this wedding is going to cost, it is time to get real. Lean into the crap that is coming up in your engagement and resolve to work it out now, not after the wedding. The way you communicate, problem-solve, and handle your shit paves the way for the years after your wedding. If you are an astute budgeter and your partner is really hoping for a lavish wedding that spares no expense, you might feel like the path of least resistance is the best one. Why argue, right? This is the time to be happy, right? It would feel horrible to burst their bubble of the wedding they've always wanted, right? WRONG. This is the time to work on the real stuff that's going to carry you as a couple: honest communication, making hard decisions together, and compromise.

your wedding is (allegedly) the one day you get to call the shots and have things play out exactly as you envision. Why though? Why can't people be the bosses of their lives every day?

Megan Ford is a clinic director, therapist, and researcher at the University of Georgia's ASPIRE Clinic. She attests that social media fundamentally affects weddings. "One of the biggest things we're seeing lately is the visibility of weddings. It has grown exponentially from social media. Weddings used to be for ourselves and our families, and that's often not the case anymore. Our weddings are visible to our larger communities and extended social network. There is this idea that everyone is watching, not just the people actually in attendance, which creates this frenzy."[18]

Ford advocates for a reality check of what's actually real. "What we see as an average wedding in a magazine or on social media might be anything but. What we're aspiring to attain might be impossible. Literally impossible. Social media just bloats this feeling that perfection should be attainable. That leads to feelings of a lot of conflict and discontentment. If you feel like you can't attain what you're always dreaming to make out of this day because the narratives that have surrounded you are so sensationalized, you're going to end up feeling disappointment and frustration. It's going to take you out, and this is the sad thing, it takes you out of what we're meant to celebrate at a wedding: Two lives and two families coming together. We lose that meaning when we focus on one fleeting day. It is a very special event, but it is one day. It is a short day."

Crystal agrees. "If we could do it all over again, oh man, because it is one day, I don't know if I would have done it," she admits. She explains that their wedding precluded them from hypothetical other things, like living in a newer or bigger house, or the opportunity to take an extended honeymoon. "So many people said to me after their weddings and before mine, they'd say 'it is just one day.' I knew I would always wonder if I didn't but now that I'm on the other side I get it. I think back to the day we got our marriage licence. We met each other on our lunch break and went to city hall, it was a gorgeous sunny day downtown. I remember thinking this afternoon is perfect. It's just us. This is what it's about."[19]

PLANNING YOUR CEREMONY

The marriage ceremony, as we know it in the Perfect White Western Wedding, is sexist beyond measure. The bride enters as something to behold, literally an object, wearing a dress that represents her purity. Her father might walk her down the aisle and "give her away" to her groom, a piece of property that moves from her father to her soon to-be-husband.

The officiant, typically a man, gives the approval for the husband to kiss the bride, as if she has no agency in the kiss. She *receives* her husband's kiss.

Later, at the reception, traditionally only men speak, while the bride is silent (and gracious, and beautiful). She will take on her husband's surname. Though to look at the colossal bridal industry machine, it is clear that the wedding is about her. She is to labour over every detail to ensure that it is her day.

That's messed up. Your wedding ceremony matters and it's high time that couples start to reclaim them.

Vowing to Love, Honour, and Obey — Wait, Back Up

When the ketubah is read during a Jewish the ceremony, it recites the terms of a contract that the couple is entering into, which confirms the man's acquisition of the woman, and protects the rights of the woman. "As far as Jewish law is concerned, under every chuppah an acquisition takes place," said Dr. Harry Freedman, contributor to the *Jewish Chronicle*. It's not for nothing that the ketubah was originally designed to protect women from being abandoned by their husbands or forced to divorce against their will. While many traditionally observant Jews continue to use the ketubah's original text, others have adapted it to be more inclusive. (Shout-out to interfaith and same-sex ketubah's, too.)

In 2008, the Muslim Institute released a modernized marriage contract. It took years of extensive research to come up with the new agreement, and it was quickly endorsed by the Muslim Parliament of Great

Britain, and the Muslim Women's Network. Prior to this, the Islamic marriage ceremony (nikkah), performed by an imam in the presence of two witnesses, involved little or no paperwork, and wasn't always recognized under civil law. If the marriage were to go awry and the couple divorced, the woman was often unable to secure the financial rights guaranteed to her under sharia law.[20] The new marriage contract helps to equalize this by clarifying both the husband's and the wife's rights and obligations in all eventualities. The contract isn't just about the marriage dissolving, though. It also helps couples galvanize their relationship by laying out the terms and conditions of the marriage and seeing where they sit on various issues.

There Is a Way to Include Everyone in Your Ceremony

One couple made every single one of their guests part of the ceremony. The rings were put into his grandmother's handkerchief. The rings were then passed around to every guest to hold and "bless" in a way. This meant that guests were participants in the ceremony, not just there as spectators. Lovely, right?

When marriage was essentially a contract, the vows were the terms. The terms of the contract were pretty straightforward, as Dr. Andrea O'Reilly, professor in the School of Gender, Sexuality, and Women's Studies at York University, explains. "Historically, marriage served as a contract — women were vulnerable financially, they needed cultural and legal protection. Marriage gave them that. In return, the husband got domesticity and children." Romantic, right? If you are familiar with the vow to "love, honour, and obey," this is a throwback to the contract that marriage once was. Even the Royals are breaking from tradition, and we all know how much these guys love tradition. Duchesses Kate Middleton and Meghan Markle both omitted the terms "to obey" from their vows, though Princess Diana trailblazed that back in 1981.[21] She broke royal precedent by deciding to not promise to obey Prince Charles.

Queen Elizabeth II, Princess Margaret, Princess Anne and generations of royal brides before them all included "obey" in their wedding vows, as dictated by the *Anglican Book of Common Prayer*, dating from 1662.

Modernizing Vows

Vows matter deeply and should be prioritized early in your planning. Getting to vows that you're comfortable with might actually take some time and discussion. They can be complicated, hard, and loaded, but they don't have to be. Some traditional vows do rear their heads in modern wedding ceremonies, but those are not written in stone.

Even if you set aside the patriarchally charged vows from years past, you are still entering into a contract of sorts. Why else are you marrying, then? Weddings mark a formal commitment. You are merging your life with another and your vows are what you say, what your partner hears, and what everyone present witnesses. Set aside for a moment the idea that your wedding is a party or celebration (of course it is). Your vows are really the thing. This is what it's about, the commitment you're making to each other, the terms of your agreement. If something doesn't feel good to you, if there is an imbalance in your vows or they just feel generic, get out your pen. Don't spend more time picking out your wedding outfit than combing through the words that are a lifelong promise.

Your wedding should be reflective of you as a couple. If your faith imparts a certain set of vows during the ceremony, but you also want to put your own stamp on things, don't hesitate to combine the two. Discuss this with your officiant so they understand your goal. If your officiant includes the traditional "who gives this woman to be married to this man?" you could just take it out and instead replace it with a few lines acknowledging your family and how much they mean to you as a couple. If they don't support this, do you want them marrying you? If you and your love are of different faiths, why not incorporate both into your ceremony?

You don't have to script every word of your entire ceremony, but you should make it meaningful — however that looks for you. Your vows, readings, and music during your ceremony should move you. Don't participate in or settle for anything less than that.

MARRYING TRADITIONS:
E AND G BLENDED THEIR BACKGROUNDS

I'm Jewish and my husband is Italian. We decided on a non-denominational wedding but added elements from our backgrounds. We were married by a judge, who happened to be a family member (my mom was her flower girl). We had a hora (because they are so fun) and had Jordan almonds at the gift table with the envelope (or busta) box. We served a pasta course and served cannoli and rugelach with an espresso bar. It felt like a great mash-up of who we are as a couple.

Adding Personal Touches

Poems and song lyrics may hold a special place for you as a couple, so take them and make them your own. It may take some time to think of the right words, but you'll get there.

Also, if you are feeling the absence of a late parent or grandparent, perhaps there are love letters they wrote that you could include an excerpt from in your ceremony. If all else fails, grab a piece of treasured jewellery to tuck into your purse or pocket. It is a beautiful way to honour them.

You might ask someone to make a toast or do a reading at your ceremony as a way to include people who are really special to you but aren't in your wedding party. Give them lots of time (a few months, at least) and provide some helpful direction like how long to speak for, a general sense of what you're hoping they'll communicate or read. Don't take it the wrong way if they decline, or you sense that they desperately want to decline. Many people have a deep fear of public speaking.

MICHELLE HONOURS HER LATE FATHER

"As a kid, I never really dreamed of having a typical wedding, but the one thing I always did think about was my dad walking me down the aisle. Unfortunately, my dad died just over a year before I got married. He was sick and in the hospital the last few weeks of his life, so I was fortunate enough to be able to have some pretty meaningful talks with him. And I knew that he approved of my boyfriend at the time — in fact, he jokingly told me not to fuck it up. I don't know where the idea came from (probably an emotional story that I read online), but once we knew he wasn't going to be alive much longer, I knew what to do. One afternoon when it was just the two of us in his room, I asked him if he would write a letter to me that my mom could read out the day that I got married. He did, with the help of my mom, and it ended up being a moment that I will never forget. Yes, I cried off a lot of my makeup at my own wedding, but it was worth it to have a moment that represented him (because they were his words) at our wedding. The letter was heartfelt and funny, which showed people at the wedding who didn't get the chance to meet him exactly what he was like."

Not everyone will have the opportunity to include a deceased loved one in their big day quite like this, but if there is someone who you want to honour, don't be afraid to enlist help and to look to find a sincere and loving way to pay tribute to them — you won't regret it.

PREPARING FOR THE UNEXPECTED

If the year 2020 taught us anything, it was that anything can (and will!) change at any moment. Many couples were forced to postpone, recreate, or cancel celebrations due to Covid-19. And according to the *Evening Standard*, 64 percent of weddings were actively postponed due to the pandemic.[22] That's a lot of shifting for the $72+ billion (USD) industry.[23] And while we're hoping that that whole nightmare is behind us, one thing we can all likely agree on is that having a rainy day plan or a chill enough attitude to make a pivot will be a positive holdover from the pandemic.

Essentially, what you should be seeking here is resiliency. Which we've likely built up thanks to the fact that the reference points that we were so used to were shaken up like a snow globe. Even in good/normal times, shit happens. Venues fall through, the dress doesn't arrive or arrives in tatters, the wedding officiant gets stuck in a snowstorm (this almost happened to Michelle!), the vases for the candles/flowers break (this also happened to Michelle — thank god for industrious besties who come in with the quick replacement vases!), someone in the wedding party becomes ill, we could go on. Because the wedding ceremony and party is a delicate dance of event planning and guiding a herd of some 100 people or so, taking things with a grain of salt is a grace that will serve you well here.

Here are a few tips on how to, at the very least, be slightly prepared for the "worst":

• Try to be understanding. Hopefully whoever is breaking their side of the bargain has come to you personally to explain their situation. And hopefully they've come to you with a solution. If a photographer becomes ill, they should have an assistant or know someone else who can fill in for them. Hear them out before you freak out.

• For anything that involved you and your partner signing a contract, reread all the fine print and put your best negotiating hats on. Those contracts are binding, so there should be some sort of

Hot Tip: Don't Strap Expensive Jewellery to Animals or Children

We're not pessimistic, we're realistic. If you have a sweet child as a ring bearer, or plan to tie your rings in a bow wrapped around your dog's neck, DO NOT use the real rings. Give the real rings to someone at the altar (officiant, wedding party, witness, whoever) and use fake rings for show. Kids and dogs, while undeniably adorable, aren't always the most predictable.

reprieve or consequence for someone cancelling on you, especially last minute. Unfortunately, this may take longer than the time allotted (i.e., before your wedding day), so if you're negotiating and don't see a swift conclusion, make like a bunny and start prepping your own way out. Be scrappy and hungry for a solution.

- Wedding insurance exists. Who knew? If you have the funds in your budget, this is something to consider.
- During the pandemic many couples had smaller, intimate ceremonies (which — and we're not sure how we feel about this — The Knot team dubbed "mini-monies"), postponing their big reception until a later date, similar to a nikkah. It's kind of the best of both worlds — you get to marry your person right away, and celebrate each other at a later, hopefully less stressful, date. Also remember that you have options if you want to make things work right away — if a venue cancels, look at getting married outdoors somewhere, weather permitting, check a previous venue option, or call in a favour with a friend/family member with a beautiful house. Can you use your ceremony venue as the reception venue or vice versa? Get creative here.
- Above all else, expect there to be bumps in the road, big and small. Don't be afraid to rely on your support network, even if it's just for a quick brainstorm. A dear friend might have a fabulous substitute dress if yours goes missing or a cousin might have a great alternative idea for a booze contact. Ask away, then edit how you and your partner see fit.

FAVOURS ARE OUT AND SUNSCREEN IS IN

Favours are superfluous, time-consuming things that no one really cares about. Did you know the original wedding favour was sugar, to show how wealthy the families were? If there is sugar on the table for your guests' coffee, consider your job done. While we're over wedding favours, we are here for taking care of your guests. If you are getting married somewhere super hot, a few baskets of paper fans and sunscreen is a nice touch. If you are getting hitched in the great outdoors, some bug repellant (er, elegantly displayed) is smart. And who doesn't love popping a mint or two when they're leaving the washroom?

• •

Real-Life Wedding Stories

Tonisha and Jan met in Berlin, where both were working in the same office.

"We started dating in our mid-thirties and we always talked really openly about marriage — what we both thought about it, how we both felt about it — and we just kept the conversation going over the years. We both knew we were working toward it, but neither of us were in a rush (we don't want kids and there was no other agenda for which we first needed to be married). We were on two separate paths going in the same direction and the paths kept coming closer together until they converged, and we decided to do it — and I don't think I have ever said anything so cheesy in my entire life. Gawd.

"I did not want a wedding and Jan decidedly did want a wedding. I thought they were a waste of time and money, not just for us, but for our friends and family (particularly mine, who were spread out over six different countries, while his were just 'next door' in Prague). We had some great chats about how we wanted to celebrate, and we were both in agreement on the main points: no big ceremony, definitely not religious, small and informal, and, most importantly for me, copious amounts of very good food. Nothing will scandalize a Jamaican family more than not having enough food at a wedding. I wanted our guests to have to roll themselves home. Since we wanted to keep it really simple, it was fairly easy to make our decisions together, but we both researched and came up with suggestions and vetoed and discussed. It wasn't me doing all the work and just presenting my ideas to Jan — he was very particular about some things!

"We both gave a solid 'hell no' to any religious elements, a long ceremony, anything overly romantic, a big white wedding dress (I wore gold); walking down the aisle with everyone staring at me, my father 'giving me away,' basically all the very traditional things.

"The things that felt like us were this: We both walked in together holding hands. We found the best wedding ceremony guy who did a funny, sweet 20-minute ceremony and suggested we do this thing where we put our rings on a piece of string which was strung around all our guests and, before each guest passed the rings to the next guest, they would silently say a wish for us as a couple. We thought that was a really sweet way of including our guests and people really loved it. Annoyingly, when it was his turn to make a wish on our rings, my father loudly exclaimed that he wished for twin grandchildren. My father knows that we do not want kids.

"We had two weddings, technically. Because we are both foreigners in Germany, the land that invented bureaucracy, we first went for a romantic weekend getaway to Denmark (quickie wedding paradise) to officially tie the knot in a ceremony that took, literally, three minutes. My first words as a married woman were, "Is that it?" We took public transportation all done up in our fancy clothes and took hilarious selfies while people stared at us; after the three minute ceremony, a random Italian tourist did an impromptu photo shoot that produced some fantastic photos. We walked around the city taking selfies and people shouted 'Congratulations!' to us in English and Danish. The night of, we went to dinner at a nice restaurant that gave us free oysters and champagne. It was lovely and we were happy that we could do this part just for us, but still get to celebrate with family later on.

"For the actual wedding, we kept it small, 40 people exactly, most of whom were family and about six good friends each, who each brought their partners. Our very good friends Caroline and Tobias have a great restaurant in Berlin called Muse, which we love, and we did everything there — the little ceremony and then the dinner. The place has a really great vibe, so we didn't do much by way of decoration.

"We called it the JamCzech wedding because I'm Jamaican and Jan is Czech. For the seating, we had four big, long tables called Germany, Canada (because I am also a proud Canadian), Jamaica, and Czech Republic. We used the food to celebrate our two cultures, so for example, jerk chicken is a popular dish in Jamaica and goulash is a popular dish in the Czech Republic, so we did Jerk Goulash. Pretty much everything was a melding of the two cultures like this — Caroline went all out on the research! We had two signature cocktails, the 'Old Jamaican,' made with Appleton Rum, and the 'Bohemian,' made with Becherovka. (They kept the latter on the restaurant's bar menu even after, and I was highly offended that my Jamaican one wasn't chosen.)

"Our wedding ceremony guy (truly I don't know what his actual title is) was hilarious and amazing. He had spent three hours interviewing us over wine a few weeks prior to the wedding and he put together something whimsical, funny, and very sweet. He was so good, people thought he was a good friend of ours. We were like naw, we found him online.

"Then we STUFFED OUR FACES! At least, our guests did; thank goodness we'd had a full menu tasting, since we didn't really eat much at the actual event. At each table, they left the head of the table free so we could move around and sit at different tables. Basically, it was just a really fun, LOUD (we got noise complaints from all the laughing), yummy delicious dinner with friends and family. We had no speeches! We cut a delicious cake of which each layer was different. There was a little dance floor downstairs where a bunch of us went later in the night and I ended up DJing my own wedding. Everyone was so stuffed they could not move from their seats, like those snakes that eat a cow and just have to sit there for a month. It was the best thing ever."

3 The Wedding-Industrial Complex

It's a Dirty Business

The wedding industry plows ahead as if feminism never happened. The past decades have seen women demand to be seen as more than how they look, more than their ability to be a wife or mother. And yet, conversely, during the exact same time has risen what sociologists have dubbed the wedding-industrial complex: a billion-dollar machine that is obsessed with and fetishizes how women look, as a gateway to being a wife and mother. Despite every hard-earned gender equity win, the wedding day continues to be the day that women are supposed to look forward to, prepare for, dream about, and spend money on, like no other day in their lives. A one-dimensional way to be a bride has completely permeated our culture.

If you've ever flipped through a bridal magazine, you've seen perfectly posed pictures of the "ideal wedding" ad nauseam. You know the one. British countryside setting. Classic calligraphy-covered floral or woodsy invitations. A big white tent. A big white gown. Ivory-clad toddlers sporting baby-pink sashes. And throw in a church as old as time for good measure. Or maybe there's a barn, swanky hotel, stately museum, or quaint garden. The space is lit by twinkly fairy lights, softly by tea lights, or perhaps by artfully hung Edison bulbs. Bridesmaids wear $300 dresses, holding matching (or very, very purposefully mismatched) bouquets. It certainly all looks beautiful, but they start to look really identical, too. Maybe there is a cheeky hashtag, or chalkboards listing his-and-hers cocktails. Here's the thing, though: the wedding industry is fuelled by the big white-wedding fantasy. It has no incentive to tell the stories that do not fit into this mould, because it doesn't profit from them. So don't try to fit that mould. Make your own.

This couple took notes on what they didn't want their wedding to look like! "A few years before Dustin proposed, there was a short period where we attended about five different weddings. All of those weddings, as fun as they were, we couldn't tell them apart. They were pretty much the same: ceremony, white dresses, matching bridesmaids' dresses, cliché speeches, even mostly the same DJ song lists. So we decided if we were going to get married it had to be different. We wanted it to be a party our friends and family would enjoy and remember, that we just happened to get married at.

"A Halloween wedding was 100 percent the only option. We love Halloween, we love horror movies, goth decor, fall, jack-o'-lanterns, bats, ghosts, fog machines, and the "Monster Mash." Nothing else would feel right. Everyone seems excited about being able to wear a costume to a wedding. Some people are keeping their costumes a secret. Everyone thinks the wedding is a perfect fit for us and who we are. We're keeping it as low budget as we reasonably can. Our venue is a family members' property, and the majority of our friends are creative types, so we have all hands on deck for planning decor without needing to hire outside help."

For every cool city hall wedding, where the couple wears exactly what they want, there are about 10 of these whitewashed weddings packaged in the media — especially with the rise of the celebrity wedding photo albums online and highly stylized affairs proliferating all over our Instagram feeds. It can leave couples feeling like they must prescribe to this same type of celebration. And it can also leave them feeling major anxiety pangs to Just. Get. It. Right.

FEELING THE PRESSURE TO DO THINGS "RIGHT"

What is right, exactly? The machine that is the wedding industry is always peddling the same message: spend, spend, spend, because this is how you demonstrate to the world that you are worthy. The message of the black hole that is bridal culture is that this is your one chance to show the world that worthiness. Be as beautiful, desirable, thin, fit, happy, and popular as possible. In the wedding fantasy, there is no room for relationship hurdles, estranged families, or less-than-middle-classness. No one seems to give a hoot about etiquette, but when there's a wedding in the works, the expectation is that we've all graduated with a master's in decorum from Good Taste University. There is certainly no room for austerity in weddings.

Let's put a few things in perspective: In North America alone, the wedding industry is a behemoth worth over $70 billion (USD) a year.[24] Estimates suggest that number balloons to around $300 billion (USD) worldwide.[25] Data from fashion site Lyst reports that 23 percent of brides buy two outfits for their big day, while the average cost of a wedding dress is up 12 percent, according to online wedding hub The Knot. That's a lot of money. And the idea that you have to dip into your savings just to have this "picture-perfect" day is outdated and old-fashioned. It doesn't add up.

Would you rather have money to put a down payment on a place to live and still have a very raucous throw down? Or are you going to

LOVE (AND MARRIAGE) IN REAL LIFE

Even years after her wedding, Sheila was left feeling a certain way about how things went down. "Looking back at my wedding, there was this consumer bullying going on. This pressure and comparison, like, 'Well, I have to do my wedding like THIS because I've seen a wedding like THAT.' Do I regret my wedding? No. But do I think about what it would have been like if we just ran off to city hall? All the time! That is so romantic. That is truly just for the couple."

A and R learned how to keep things simple, just how they wanted. "We met, we got engaged really quickly within a year, and on our one-year anniversary of being together we moved to Dubai. We lived in Dubai for four years pretending to be married, it was easier (it was technically illegal for us to live as an unmarried couple). We planned on going for one year and stayed for four. We waited until we got home to Canada to get married. I was working in events in Dubai and doing really elaborate productions. When the time came to plan our wedding, it felt right to move away from the extreme luxury I had become used to. I wanted something small and simple.

"We got married in the restaurant where we had our first date. It was 50 people and we bucked every trend. No dancing. Very few speeches. We served a 10-course dinner with the DJ playing throughout. We just really wanted to do something that was fun for us. Luckily, our parents totally trusted us, given my profession. In hindsight, the fact that we were living abroad made it easier to keep our numbers low, as we planned it from afar. It was a sort of unnecessary formality for us, but we're so glad we did it. I found being a bride a bit weird. I felt really strange trying on wedding dresses. I went to university with Canadian designer Lucian Matis and asked him to make me something as he knew my style and personality. He sent me a sketch, I fully trusted him, and a week before the wedding, I tried it on. The pomp and circumstance of trying on dresses with a group of friends isn't me, I didn't want to be over-celebrated. Some people love it, but for me it just didn't feel right. Staying true to yourself is a big part of the process."

spend, spend, spend, for one day's worth of fun? Whatever your pleasure, have at it. No matter where you land, you don't need to succumb to any pressures that you're feeling. You can be woke on your wedding day (by saying no to things that don't feel authentic to you), not go broke, *and* still have the wedding of your dreams.

Your day can still be special. It can still be one of the best days of your life. Your wedding day will still have meaning, to you, your partner, and your family and friends. Because it's about you two agreeing to something really special — being each other's partners for as long as you can stand each other, or death does you part.

ONE BRIDE'S PERILOUS STORY GOES TOO FAR

"Our wedding was 120 people in Florida at a country club that my husband and his family belong to. The club opened a week early for us, so our guests had the run of the place. It was like five weddings in one, because we organized daily dinners and brunches. We also had tons of group activities, coordinated travel to and from the airport, golf, tennis, even arranging blowouts.

"It wasn't a huge wedding, but for a destination wedding it was massive. And, it certainly wasn't a turnkey destination wedding. Everything had to be designed.

"I worked in the bridal industry for years. The commercialization of the wedding industry was too much. By the time I was planning my wedding, I was over it. I wanted to get married in Vegas by Jewish Elvis.

"My now-husband didn't want to elope. We went to visit this country club right after we got engaged. It looked stunning. Gorgeous southern estate, dripping in Spanish moss; the air smelled like orange groves. We ripped around in golf carts, it was a blast.

"At the time, the Canadian to U.S. dollar exchange was really favourable — we could do a lot with a little. But, we (i.e., me) had to plan out every single detail. It was elaborately orchestrated. It was all about our guests' experience. I had to meet with the caterer, the event staff, babysitters, everyone. We had dietary restrictions, travel delays, and tidal waves of questions from guests to attend to.

"My MIL likes to take charge. She flew down to Florida six weeks before the wedding and met with the wedding planner, caterer, and florist. She changed a bunch of stuff. I got an awkward call from the wedding planner to tell me how uncomfortable she felt. It was a pain, and I had to undo her changes. Some things I let go (she changed the configuration of the ceremony, which I didn't care enough to change back). She added a head table at the reception that we didn't want, but we just rolled with it.

"At some point, I stopped talking to her directly, and was communicating through my husband. I was really trying to delicately balance wanting to get off on the right foot, go along to get along. A wedding is a day, marriage is a lifetime, but in hindsight it would have been a great time to draw some boundaries.

"If I could go back and talk to my bright-eyed, newly engaged self, I'd tell her to practise saying no. Because it doesn't serve to say yes. No can be a complete sentence and you don't have to qualify it with anything else. The advice I would give to brides is to be gracious but firm. Your new family is to be respected, but not at the expense of your well-being. It's one day.

"I felt so uncomfortable being the centre of attention, so in a way, I could deflect that by letting my MIL run with things. All of these people come together for you to celebrate you and your love. It is easy to feel overwhelmed by that, you feel yourself on this precipice of this great life change, yet everyone is looking at you.

"Was it the wedding I wanted? Look, it was a dream wedding, but my dream was never a big wedding. But there were some principles that had to happen: Everyone felt special, everyone felt taken care of, everyone had a great time. I married the guy that I love in a beautiful place."

ACKNOWLEDGING THE PINK WORK OF THE WEDDING BUSINESS

Marriage, family, and the general emotional well-being of everyone has traditionally been (and, let's be real, still very much is) women's work. The wedding industry has been slow to evolve from those values. Socially, we approach marriage as if women want the wedding and they must get the guy to come around in order for them to fulfill their singular goal in life: The Perfect Wedding. Article titles include "15 Psychological Tricks to Make Him Propose,"[26] "Will He Ever Marry You? Getting Your Guy to Propose,"[27] "5 Ways to Get Your Partner to Propose,"[28] and "How to Get Him to Propose and Marry You Without Looking Low Value."[29] *Glamour* published a recipe for "engagement chicken" to hook him into marriage.

This narrative feeds the myth that men are passive, incidental bystanders in this: get him to propose then get on with planning that wedding. The framework has been: ensure there is a proposal (women's work), propose (men's work), plan the wedding and every detail within an inch of its life (women's work), live happily ever after, the end. But, thank goodness, times are changing.

Planning a wedding is often gendered and it is most often (in heterosexual couples) the woman who is deciding what the priorities are. Of course, by necessity, LGBTQ+ couples really tend to buck these tired old heteronormative roles when it comes to wedding planning, unless one part of the duo feels more apt performing certain duties. But when it comes to weddings of cisgendered, heterosexual couples, Megan Ford, M.S., LMFT, clinic director, financial therapist, and financial therapy researcher at the University of Georgia's ASPIRE Clinic attests that "men haven't often been socialized in the same way to normalize wedding planning, so women often feel much more attuned to what it is going to take to pull off a wedding now days." She points out that this is problematic because some women might not want to take on the labour of planning a wedding and some men might not speak up if they don't agree with where things are moving because they don't feel it is their place to.

For those whose actual business is weddings, there is still immense pressure. Josh Spiegel, Creative Director at NY-based Birch Event Design, suggests that if couples think they feel the pressure for perfection, those in the industry feel it on an entirely new level. "The wedding industry is insanely intense. I always second-guess myself. Did I get this idea because it is really good, or because I had to get a proposal out of the door?" He says that Sundays are the worst day because he goes on Instagram to look at weddings from the previous night. "I look at everyone's wedding and think 'This is gorgeous, and my work will never compare to this.'" He describes the competition as being savage. "You could have created the best wedding yesterday, and tomorrow come out with something so mediocre; then people think that was your best work. You want people to think you did killer work. It must be excellent."[30]

Joan DiFuria is the co-founder and director of Money, Meaning & Choices Institute in California. She holds degrees in education and psychology, and a licence in marriage, family, and child counselling. She points out that when girls are already being bombarded with images of wedding iconology they are too young to get just what it is: fiction. "The fantasy of the wedding is societally normalized from such a young age, particularly for young girls. From the age of two or three, girls are taught to build this up as the moment of your life, and before the age of nine years old we don't have the capacity to think abstractly," she explains. "So kids are taking this fantasy in, lock, stock, and barrel. It isn't until much later that we can psychologically contextualize this societal and cultural pressure, and by then it is so deeply ingrained."[31]

Though conventional weddings drip with gender stereotypes, same-sex marriages, multicultural weddings, and involved grooms are shaking things up. The book *A Groom's Guide to Surviving a Wedding: One Groom's True Story*[32] advises that it is incumbent upon grooms to be involved, but, make no mistake, weddings are for the bride. According to author Jim Cutter, "This is a day where the groom will be slightly less than the better half; probably around 5 percent or so. The wife gets the diamond ring, the bridal shower(s), the registry, etc. You get nothing.

Luckily for you, in exchange for all of that, she's going to be doing most of the wedding planning." Cutter goes on to (wisely) advise men to stay close to their other half on the planning. "That doesn't mean you let her do it alone, though. And there are a few good reasons why you shouldn't. The first one is that it's your wedding, too."

Therapist Steven Giles is of the same mind. For a marriage to be a healthy one, right from the jump, one person singularly planning the wedding is a washout. "The mindset has to be 'you're my priority and I'm your priority,' and what that means is that you have to stand up for me and protect me," he explains. "So, in many cases, organizing a marriage or not, when the spouse is being treated like an outsider from the other and isn't being protected, then that person will feel like they can't trust you, which leads to conflicts of whether or not the partner loves the other or if that partner can protect them in times of danger."[33] Yikes. A good gut check is to keep in mind that while you're planning a wedding, you're also laying down the tracks for your marriage.

A *Huffington Post* article by one soon-to-be-married man echoes the need for both people getting married to be involved in the planning.

> "Girls just care more about this stuff," said a male friend of mine recently whose now-wife planned pretty much his entire wedding, despite the fact that she works long hours at a high-stress job. My male friend is right — a lot of the time, women legitimately care more. But not 500 percent more, which is about how much more work they do than most of us.[34]

Weddings aren't women's business. Weddings are the business of the two people getting married. And yet, we're reminded that weddings are not only for brides to plan, but for their mothers and mothers-in-law, too.

MODERNIZING OUT-OF-DATE THINKING

The Wedding Book: The Big Book for Your Big Day by Mindy Weiss and Lisbeth Levine has been a perennial book on shelves for more than 10 years. The back of the book has pages of little pre-written stickers that read, "Talk to Mom." Come again? Not, "Talk to the person you are marrying, the only other person who is actually implicated in your wedding day." Talk to your mom?

Changing Your Name ... or Not!

Dime-a-dozen wedding-planning worksheets and countless apps flag reminders to "Change your name!" assuming that brides will take their husband's surname. One book concedes that many women (the author herself included) "can't wait to take on a new married name," but some women might feel that if they established themselves at work "they might be loath to tamper with their professional standing." What if it has nothing to do with a woman's career? What about someone wanting to keep their name because changing it feels out of touch with their values? Heaven forbid the word *feminist* (Gasp! The sound of pearls being clutched round the world) appears in the context of a wedding planning.

A study published in the journal *Gender Issues* reported that more than 70 percent of American adults believe that a woman should change her name after she is married.[35] What's more (hope you're sitting down for this part), about half feel that it should be *required by law*. According to a 2017 *Maclean's* article by Anne Kingston, "more than half of Canadian Millennials and Gen Xers believe a married couple should share the same name (while fewer than half of Boomers do)" and 99 percent of those people said they thought it should be the husband's last name that is shared.

Like most "traditions" around weddings, the idea of becoming Mrs. Husband's Name is a phenomenon of the last 150 years or so. Stephanie Coontz, author of *Marriage, a History: How Love Conquered*

WHITEWASHING MAY BE ERASING AFRICAN WEDDING CULTURE

Dr. Lindani Mbunyuza-Memani's work explores how Blackness is erased from weddings in South Africa.[*] She explains that Black South Africans generally celebrate two types of weddings, one white (big white Western wedding style) and the second a traditional South African wedding. These traditional or ethnic weddings are premised on African cultural beliefs and traditions in which the wedding party and guests generally dress in traditional clothing rather than the more European style of dress that is associated with white weddings — i.e., white bridal gowns and suits. Dr. Mbunyuza-Memani analyzed South African wedding reality programs, like *Our Perfect Wedding* and *Top Billing Weddings*, and found that traditional weddings are diminished, with the focus on a white wedding. She also noted that natural Black hair is erased, as the shows consistently feature brides with chemically processed or store-bought hair rather than natural hair. "Black brides assimilate themselves to white looks, a process that is connected to consumerism to suggest that Blackness is connected to frugality and ugliness in wedding spaces," argues Dr. Mbunyuza-Memani.

What's particularly concerning is that there is a cycle of sameness here. Television continues to produce what sells, so as the narrative of the white wedding is championed in place of traditional weddings, more shows perpetuate this outdated ideal. The media reproduce what has

---

[*] Lindani Mbunyuza-Memani, "Wedding Reality TV Bites Black: Subordinating Ethnic Weddings in the South African Black Culture," *Journal of Communication Inquiry* 42 , no. 1 (January 1, 2018: 26–47).

worked elsewhere to ensure profits, and this reproduction of sameness negates cultural differences (down with the melting pot theory). This is where things get homogenized, which is important, as South Africans have long been exposed to foreign produced wedding reality TV shows like *Whose Wedding Is It Anyway?*, *Destination Weddings*, and *Big Fat Gypsy Weddings*. Unfortunately for many, these shows establish a binary where there is a superior, indelible, and universal white wedding (that requires all the couples' energy) versus an "inferior" traditional wedding. The white wedding is tied to a higher social status and normalized as better, while the ethnic wedding is represented as a disposable feature of Blackness, which we all know is just not true.

Marriage, argues that this developed in the 19th century, as a sort of trendy American form.[36] By the end of the century, a woman taking her husband's name in the form of Mrs. His Name was widely adopted. Women were viewed by and defined by their marital status. Spoiler alert: Not every woman was into it and it took another century before Ms. was introduced — an equivalent to Mr., as it applies at any age, married or unmarried.

Stereotyping and All Its Pitfalls

The Knot, the incredibly popular bridal magazine, now website, has been criticized for continuing to push old-fashioned values and gender roles that are tone-deaf to a lot of couples, most recently in a *New York Times* feature.[37]

Melissa Bach, a senior director of public relations for The Knot Worldwide, which also includes WeddingWire, said the company recently made some updates to its website, app, social media, and emails.[38] This included, she said, changing the phrase "bridal party" to "wedding party" and showcasing photos of same-sex couples. Last year, The Knot also changed the name of its proposal site from "How He Asked" to "How They Asked." "While we've taken many steps toward being more inclusive, we know that we're not perfect and there's always more we can be doing to be better," Bach said.

For Dr. Chrys Ingraham, professor of sociology at Purchase College at State University of New York, change can't come fast enough. She points out that the wedding industry is slow to change for millions of dollars — er, we mean reasons. "It is a multi-million-dollar industry with huge global economic connections and an ideological foundation that is secured throughout popular culture from toys to films to romance."[39] This shit goes deep. "If one understands the history of marriage and weddings, it is very apparent that institutionalized heterosexuality forms the foundation of wedding practices from marketing to ritual. Marriage historically privileges the privileged, providing access to everything from health benefits to social security. Participating in everything from a marriage licence to going on a honeymoon resecures the institution regardless of the sex of the participants." Though anyone can (and should be able to) marry who they choose, Ingraham makes the case that "mimicking the ritual does not displace it but reifies it." While gay marriage opens up access, it still does so in a restricted environment, making it operate on the margins of a patriarchal society.

While Ingraham doesn't mince words about her stance on weddings ("abolish the wedding industry" she deadpans), she encourages couples to rip up the rule book. "Don't participate. Develop your own rituals that involve social priorities rather than egocentric ones. Build a wheelchair ramp together; host a fundraiser for people in need; have a potluck. Get over yourself."

And we tend to agree with her. Although it may seem extreme, the wedding-industrial complex really does need a massive overhaul. (Hello! That's why we're here.) But one thing we will 100 percent stand by is that this can all be on a spectrum, depending on what matters most to the couple doing the actual marrying. Edit according to your paradigm and your wishes.

The cultural assumptions mentioned above (i.e., taking the husband's last name, the work of the wedding falling on the shoulders of the woman) keep us stuck. They become the part of the script that we're all supposed to follow. Let's keep pushing for progress, shall we? If one is participating in a ritual or a practice, we think it's incumbent upon them to know about it and decide if it is right for them. We're not against tradition (unless it's sexist, homophobic, racist, or otherwise divisive, then we're against your tradition), but we are for conscious, informed decision-making.

People of Honour

One of the easiest ways to stick to the wedding industry's outdated value system is to create a wedding party that speaks to people who are truly your friends and confidantes, regardless of gender. We absolutely adore seeing a couple with non-gender-specific people as their attendants. Yes, men and women can be platonic friends, so having a good pal stand up for you regardless of how they identify is truly glorious, and modern AF.

Masculinizing the Couple's Speech

Have you ever thought it was a little weird that only the groom addressed the room at the wedding and the bride sat there silently with a polite smile on her face? Full disclosure, Michelle didn't speak at her wedding, but that was because the day was pretty emotional for her and she was extremely nervous about blubbering through something and sounding insincere. But what has been tradition for a long-ass time is that the groom says a few words while the bride does not.

And why is that? This is 100 percent a holdover from when men spoke on behalf of their wives. A 2017 study by wedding planning app Bridebook, only 12 percent of brides surveyed actually made speeches at their own wedding.[40] Further to that, the expectation of who will speak at the wedding leans heavily on the male contingent. Of a group of almost 1,700 people surveyed in Great Britain, only 16 percent believed that the bride should make a speech, as opposed to 51 percent for grooms.[41]

If you're someone who enjoys a great public speaking moment and would relish doing so, stand firm and have your say.

Giving Me Away, What?

For some women, the act of being walked down the aisle by their dads is emotional and a testament to their relationships. For others, they feel off being given away. Whether you feel it is sweet or strange to be walked down the aisle by dear old dad is up to you, but any bride saying yes to that should know where the custom comes from.

Sadly, it's not so sweet, explains Dr. O'Reilly. This portion of the ceremony exists to attest that "the bride went from her father directly to her husband, and that no man had come between them. It was guaranteeing her virginity."[42] What's more, it was likely that the bride was a sort of currency, for the father to maybe pay off a debt or grab another rung on the social ladder. While we can all agree that *Father of the Bride* is an excellent film, the tradition of the father (or heck, anyone, really) giving the bride away is a barbaric little holdover from days gone by.

Lots of brides are walking their own fine asses down the aisle (we see you walking that first half of the aisle, Meghan Markle), with their beloved, with both mom and dad, or just doing whatever feels right to them — as should you. Feel free to amend this part of the ceremony entirely. To create more parity, why not do that for both people getting married? An even wilder idea: you can both walk down the aisle together as a couple.

Freeing Yourself from Unwelcome Conventions

Receiving lines: Perfect wastes of time. Literally no one likes them.

The garter toss: The garter toss is vulgar. A piece of your lingerie is getting hurled into a crowd of dudes who fight over it. Scrap that, and the bouquet toss while you're at it. All these things do is single out the singles at your wedding. Trust us: They are well aware that they are single. They are at a wedding FFS.

The first dance: Unless the two of you are super stoked about it, don't feel pressure to do it. It is really awkward to have a slow dance with a room of people watching you. Where do you look?! Into your partner's eyes THE ENTIRE SONG? Skip it. Unless you have some Bruno Mars moves — then share that gift with the world.

Kissing on demand: When people start clinking their glasses to get you two to kiss, don't do it. If you do it once, this is positive reinforcement and it will last all night. It is like feeding pigeons in the park. Once you start, you'll be swarmed. You could ask your emcee to advise that the happy couple will not be kissing on demand tonight, so please no clanging of glasses, pounding of tables, bad singing at the podium, etc.

Limousines: This is a surplus expense if we've ever heard of one. Get your people where they need to be on time, but go for a cheaper (and if we're honest, more elegant) option like a few town cars. Or hell, taxis or upgraded Ubers.

Having "sides" for seating: The point here is that you're merging families! Blend, people, blend!

Favours: Just no.

Not seeing each other the night before the wedding: Er, we're going to hazard a guess that those 40 percent of marriages that end in divorce didn't end up that way because the couple hung out before the wedding. Do what is practical, but what's better than snuggling up with your honey the night before you marry? NOTHING IN THE WORLD.

Real-Life Wedding Stories

L and B were in their mid-30s when they met, and they moved in together after eight months. They were engaged after one year.

"We had our wedding at the bar where we had our first date. We knew the owners and were friendly with them. We called them to book it, told them to get some cheese plates and booze, and said we'd bring some cupcakes. We found an officiant that had married some friends, a secular hippie lady in a robe.

"We told everyone that we were going to get married at city hall and that this was our engagement party. It was friends and first family — no extended family. The only people who knew that it wasn't an engagement party and that it was actually our wedding were the out-of-towners, as they likely wouldn't have otherwise made the trip. Not even our parents, siblings, or best friends knew. One of my best friends, who wears dresses every day of her life, wore jeans to our wedding. The one day she wore jeans … She was mortified.

We managed to keep the secret by just really convincing ourselves that this was the story. The trick to good lying is to believe the story yourself. So when my mom would bug me, 'When are you booking city hall? I want to buy a new dress, blah blah,' I was like 'Relax, relax, we will, we will!'

"I never cared about the wedding part. I wanted a part-ner and a family but never cared about the big thing. I went one afternoon to a department store, booked the private shopping room, and bought a gorgeous cocktail dress, not even super fancy. I bought some new shoes. [...] My husband had one suit and one tie. He was like, 'I'm just going to wear this thing.' [The night before the wedding] I ran out and got him a tie, and to this day those are the only two ties he owns.

"At the time, I was working at a magazine and there was a guy in the photo department who did some photography on the side. We got him to come and just take some candid shots. We didn't want the posed shit.

"On the day of the wedding, we went for dim sum, went and looked at a couch — standard weekend fare. I had booked a hotel room for the night to be special and got a hair and makeup person to get me ready. I went over to the hotel to meet them and a few friends who came in from out of town.

"[My husband's] dad gave us some money for the party. My parents threw us an engagement party before our fake engagement party. So, my mom did her speeches, all the things that she really wanted to do.

"My mom would have driven me wild wanting the big Jew-do. It would have been a nightmare for my husband, who is so shy, to have all these people looking at him, none of whom he knows. That was the right way to get married, for us. It was about getting to do things the way you want to do them, but also a financial practicality. We didn't have a lot of money and we wanted to buy a house. We were like, 'With what money are we going to pay for this wedding?' It would have been a big cheap wedding that I would have thought was tacky. None of it was my thing and none of it would have been something my husband enjoyed.

"If I could do it all over again, the only thing we'd change is that we would have more food. The wedding was over cocktail hour and I was hungry and then we had to order roti at the end of the night."

4 Wedding Attire
It's About Getting It Right, Not White

Wedding gowns are white, right? Well, yes, but like most trappings of the typical wedding ideal, that's a fairly recent phenomenon. Back in the day, brides weren't only practical about the size of their wedding, but also what they wore on their wedding day. Women got married in a beautiful dress (if they were lucky, a new dress, but that wasn't always the case) and often wore it again and again, altering the dress to suit whatever fashions were in style, or to fit their changing shape. Pretty much up until the 1950s, Western weddings were largely small religious affairs, without much place for pomp or pageantry. Whatever dress a

A Lot of Whites

Ever try picking out white paint? If so, you know that it is anything but simple. Try on a range of shades, from icy blue whites to warm creams. And if you aren't feeling like you want to wear any shade of white/cream/ivory, wear whatever you feel best in!

bride wore wasn't supposed to be the most beautiful or expensive garment that she would ever wear. People wanted to look nice, sure, but this chase for perfection wasn't a thing. Ask your grandmother. The good old days, indeed, eh?

Non-traditional wedding looks are now becoming all the rage. But that doesn't mean that you won't get some ire from close friends and family. For every "You're wearing what?" you'll likely get a few "Yeah, girl!" So stick with your vision on this one, because that's exactly what matters in this moment. What if you aren't feeling a white dress? What if you envision yourself getting married in a hot black cocktail dress, gorgeous red gown, or a satin tuxedo? Do iiiiiiiiit! When it comes to wedding attire, choice is way overdue. We get inundated with endless choices for everything else, yet bridal attire seems so limited. You're marrying who you want to, right? Do it in whatever outfit that makes you feel your best.

LEARNING THE HERSTORY OF THE WHITE WEDDING DRESS

There's a common assumption that white symbolizes purity, and there's a bit of that, what with patriarchy's obsession with women's virginity and controlling our sexuality. (Honeymoon sheets, anyone?) But the white is about something way more benign: One very famous bride who really, really liked lace.

Up until the early 1800s, the norm for Western brides was to get married in a nice dress, in whatever colour they liked, which for practical reasons was rarely white. Celts commonly favoured red wedding dresses because they symbolize fertility. Many brides wore black if they were marrying a widower or were widowed themselves (which was quite common). Many brides just wore the nicest dress that they had.

Then, in 1840, a 20-year-old woman shook all that up. This trendsetter — Queen Victoria, by the way — really, really loved lace. So she had her wedding gown incorporate some of the white lace that she loved so much. She started a trend that has clearly persevered. Fun fact: *she* actually proposed to her soon-to-be-groom. Somehow, the lace trend stuck and a woman asking this most auspicious question did not.

After Queen Victoria was wed wearing her now-famous white dress, white became *de rigueur*.[43] Wearing a white wedding gown wasn't just a symbol that you were trendy AF, it said that you were rich. Seriously rich. Back then, washing was done by hand, and folks weren't wearing white much. It was a completely impractical colour, as most people weren't peacocking. A white gown says, "I'm not washing this dress against a washing board. I have people to wash this thing for me." So, the lore of a white wedding dress has a little to do with fashion, a bit of snobbery, and a dose of patriarchy. In post–Second World War North America, the newly invented wedding industry crafted this notion that the white wedding dress was a crucial element, not only of some sacred ceremony but also symbolic of freedom and prosperity.

Making of a Wedding Dress

While the fantasy of the Perfect Dress has increased, the quality of most dresses has decreased. A lot.

Back when the white gown trend was taking off, brides that were donning these glorious ensembles were also wearing garments that were painstakingly made from a bespoke pattern, using the finest fabrics their wallets could buy. That's a far cry from what most commercial gowns are made from today. Fast fashion has eroded respect for how clothing is made and nowhere is that more evident than wedding dresses. See the box on the next page.

MOST DRESSES ARE MADE OF PLASTIC (AND OTHER THINGS YOU NEED TO KNOW ABOUT GOWNS!)

Fabric is made by knitting or weaving fibres together. If you look really, really closely at whatever garment you're wearing, you'll notice a tiny grid pattern. Fibres can be made from a lot of things, such as wool, cotton, or silk. Fibres can also be totally synthetic, like polyester. Synthetic fabrics are generally way cheaper, and if you do your research, most dresses hanging on the racks of bridal boutiques are going to have some (or a lot of) polyester in them. In fact, polyester or poly blends are pretty ubiquitous.

Not all poly blends are created equal — you'll notice the difference when you pick up a dress. Feel the fabric between your fingers, look at how it drapes, and pay careful attention to the seams. If it looks cheap, it probably is cheap. And there is NOTHING wrong with cheap, per se. Making sure a gown or frock is tailored to the body will help ensure it doesn't show receipts in a less flattering way.

What every bride should know is that gowns require a lot of fabric, and some engineer-grade tailoring goes into their construction. There's an art to making the fabric drape a certain way or having a waistline nip in just so. It's all pretty serious business. One of the easiest ways for mass-market designers to cut costs is to cheap out on the fabric. That's why you'll see racks and racks of polyester blends over pure silks. If you have to choose between a glamorous, elaborate gown made of polyester (aka polyethylene terephthalate, a petroleum by-product, aka plastic) or a simpler gown made from really amazing high-quality fabric, go for the latter. It will move better, feel better, and is most likely better for the environment, as it won't contribute to the unending stream of petroleum-based products that we have in the world.

Waking Up to Dress Shopping Myths

In addition to the pressure to find The Perfect Dress, there is also high-grade pressure for dress shopping to be some transcendental experience. It doesn't have to be that way, and you're not a failure if you're not ecstatic at the idea of shopping for a dress. Shopping for a wedding dress is often depicted as this incredible, special moment. The bride and her loved ones — maybe her best friends, sister(s), her mom — go into an airy, serene boutique and are served flutes of champagne. The woman slips into the fitting room, only to emerge, fully transformed into a BRIDE. The dress fits. She loves everything about how her body looks and this super symbolically charged garment that she is wearing. At the first glimpse of her, everyone in the store bursts into tears: she has found "the one" dress. Champagne toast. Done. Along with every other fantasy conjured up in the wedding machine, let this go, too.

The Importance of Knowing Your Shit

If you hear anyone talking about a wedding gown made from satin, you can get know-it-all-y because satin is a finish, not a fabric. Pure silk, cotton, polyester, or any combination thereof can have a satin finish.

I (Karen) found the pressure to find The Dress to be totally overwhelming. As soon as my partner and I announced we were getting married, the first question anyone asked me (okay, after "have you set a date?") was whether I had found a dress. The Dress is the pinnacle of the entire wedding fantasy. I felt like I lost the plot because I hadn't dreamed about a wedding dress my entire life, and I was too practical to drop the equivalent of several mortgage payments on a garment I'd wear for a few hours. The search for The Dress was this paramount aspect of planning a wedding, and my other half wasn't getting any of those same questions. What he was wearing to our wedding was apparently of no consequence.

Not only was I supposed to be lusting after a very expensive dress, there was a way to search for it. There is a method, apparently. You're supposed to go to a boutique with your friends (appointment required,

WEDDING SHOP OF HORROR (STORIES)*

Kelly, a Toronto woman, felt like a pariah for choosing a decidedly non-bridal 1970s-esque jumpsuit. "I didn't tell anyone, I just found it and loved it. I felt almost sheepish about not wanting a big gown, but I tried this on and felt strong and badass." Another woman in the store asked her if the outfit was for a bridal shower or bachelorette party. "When I told her that I was going to get married in this, it was like she watched me grow a second head." Kelly plans to wear the jumpsuit with leopard heels and a leather jacket. "I have to feel like myself. I want to eat, dance, and breathe. I don't want to feel like a mannequin." She is Greek. "I don't know how I'm going to tell my grandmother that I'm not getting married in a church or wearing a classic wedding dress. The big fat Greek wedding is a thing!"

Crystal recently got hitched and wore two dresses that day, neither of them wedding dresses. "I wore a bridesmaid dress to my wedding (this gorgeous tea-length strapless dress) and a miniskirt cocktail dress to the reception." Both dresses, together, were less than $1,000 (CDN), she says. "I wanted a 1940s-style dress and I couldn't find it as a wedding dress and that ended up being a blessing. I was looking for a deal and I didn't want the bullshit of shopping for a dress being a big time." She found the dress — er, two dresses — of her dreams.

Natalie went to a bridal boutique with her mom to try on dresses, even though she was already in the process of having a dress custom made by Canadian atelier Greta

---

* Discussions with Kelly [pseud.], Crystal, Natalie, and Alice [pseud.] and Karen Cleveland, November 2019–May 2020.

Constantine. "I just assumed, as an only child, and an only daughter, that my Mom would want that experience. I felt like I was trying on other people's dresses. None of them felt like me." She did the whole show-pony thing to just placate her mom and felt icky throughout the whole process. A waste of a few precious hours, to be sure.

Alice came to like her wedding dress, after she hated it for a few months. "I found this online retailer that sells well-priced, gorgeous dresses, but my friends wanted to create a 'thing' for dress shopping. We basically had this outing for my friends, not me. Every store gave me a hard time about shopping last minute, super high key pressure. (For the record, I shopped in February for an August wedding. Come on.) It added this extra layer of pressure to find a dress immediately, which I learned is really just a sales tactic.

"I'm not the sample size, so these strangers are clamping me into these dresses that are three or four sizes too small for me, making me feel like a sausage. It was not the rom-com experience of tearing up when you find 'the one' dress. What's more, I had ten different people's opinions in the room, so it turned into a decision by committee. At the last dress shop, I started to cry because I was exhausted. So I settle on this dress. It was way too much money. Of course, the designer of the dress just happened to be in the store that day, so they drew a picture of me in it: that's some serious *Say Yes to the Dress* bullshit.

"Fast forward a month, the dress comes in, and I hate it. I turned all red and itchy, I had a physical reaction to how much I hated it, like get-it-off-get-it-off-get-it-off. So I go back to the store, freaking out, and the staff pull me into this secret room that they NEVER showed me in the beginning, with tons of dresses in my size and at way lower price points. At this stage, I had to concede that it was a sunk cost. They'll give me back my deposit, which now means I either eat another $2,500 (CDN) and keep the dress that I currently hate, or I have to find another dress for less than $2,500.

"They pressure brides to buy a dress, then are like 'Sorry, you're stuck with it' if you have second thoughts. I could not, in good conscious, walk away from that amount of money. It's ridiculous. I kept the damn dress. I went for a second fitting and hated it less. On the day of the wedding, I actually liked it and felt really special in it."

obviously, have you not seen the movie *Bridesmaids*?!), make a day of it, blah blah.

The thing is, I don't like shopping with other people. Even for yogourt. I *really* like to shop alone. I want to decide, without the input of anyone else, whether or not I like something enough to buy it. What if I invited a few friends, my mom, and my mother-in-law and sister-in-law, and no one liked the dress that I liked best? Would I get talked into a dress because I didn't want to let other people down? Eff that.

I knew of a local designer (shout-out to Lowon Pope) who was down the street from me. I walked in, asked if they had time to see me. I came prepared with a short but non-negotiable list of requisites: no poof, no lace, no embroidery, no sparkles, and bra friendly. In 15 minutes I had a sample off-the-rack that, over the next month, was tailored to me until it basically felt like couture.

I loved wearing that dress because it felt like me in a gorgeous dress, not like I was trying to look the part of a bride. The fact that it was well-priced and helped support a local designer made it even better. The social aspect of shopping for a dress with other people didn't feel comfortable, so I just went and bought the dress without telling anyone. It was private and decadent — a little secret with myself.

Putting Yourself First

Natalie wanted to feel like herself, but an enhanced version of that. "I didn't look at wedding stuff. I looked at fashion content. I looked to old movie stars, with pintucked hair, glamorous black women. I knew I wouldn't find that in bridal magazines." When she did see beautiful Black women in bridal magazines and advertising, it felt tokenistic. "Oh! They've made an effort to be diverse. They're making a point."

Before you hit the stores (or start perusing online), think about what you feel best in. What kind of jeans do you love? What necklines do you like to wear? If you feel most like yourself in a loose, blousy shape, don't get talked into a fitted gown with a corseted bodice. You'll be miserable in it. If you're not used to going braless, your wedding is not the night for a test drive. You're going to be self-conscious all night worrying about the free state of your breasts. (Just us?) Likewise, if you rarely wear anything strapless: even the most beautifully made gown looks tacky if a bride has to put her thumbs down her armpits trying to wrestle her dress up over her bust all night. If you found a strapless gown that you love, consider asking your tailor to add some straps to it during the fitting process.

It is totally normal to feel

- entirely "meh" about shopping for a dress;
- excited about shopping for a dress;
- better shopping by yourself;
- like you want other people's opinions;
- not like yourself (like you're sort of wearing a costume or playing a part);
- not transformed or elated;

- perfectly content with a dress without feeling like it is "the one"; or
- intimidated by the environment (we have some ideas on where else to look for an outfit — stand by).

For my (Michelle's) wedding day, I wanted something that was reminiscent of the smart white ensemble my late grandmother wore to marry my grandfather. It was a longer jacket paired with a three-quarter length pencil skirt. She topped it off with a jaunty hat and a pair of killer shoes. For my big day, my mother made a few proclamations that I dare not repeat, but what surprised me most was that she didn't think my choice of look was "traditional." What could get more traditional than a riff on a look from the 1950s? To appease her, I took her to a big bridal store in the city and tried on multiple outfits with her and two of my best gals, who sat back and drank champagne while I rotated through looks. In the end, she came to realize that these dresses and gowns did not really suit me. My personal twist on my grandmother's attire (think a bit more form-fitting, with a cut-out on the back of my dress for some sex appeal when it was time to lose the jacket), was the best way for me to feel like me, and it was actually super traditional, if I do say so myself. What made it even better? My grandfather lovingly told me that I looked like his Louise when he first saw me that night.

Our advice is that if someone is giving you flack about your wedding day look, stick to your guns. While champagning and trying on dresses with my mom and friends was pretty fun, it was also pretty unnecessary. Don't be like Michelle. You don't have time for that.

Searching for Your Dress: The Bridal Boutique Universe

Walk into a popular bridal boutique and you'll likely be given the same spiel: it is best to order your dress six to nine months before your wedding and be prepared for three fittings (over eight weeks) before you take your dress home.

The average cost of a gown is around $1,700 (CDN), according to *Weddingbells* magazine,[44] with alterations running as high as 20 to 25 percent of that cost.

Ever wonder why? Because it is great for the industry and not so great for consumers. If you ask why this is the case, you'll be regaled with the beautiful fabric, the careful craftsmanship, the lining, and the actual design and fit of the dress. Maybe it is made with silk that is $150 a yard. Maybe some of the embroidery or beading is done by hand. Even if that dress has all of these bells and whistles, it still likely doesn't add up to its cost. The hidden factor behind the price is that it is a *wedding* dress. Anything wedding undeniably makes the cost go up.

What's more, bridal boutiques are heavy on the heartstrings and light on economics. You might be given a sales pitch that this is the dress you'll wear on the most important day of your life, that generations of your family will look back on photos of you in the dress. It's all emotional stuff, identical to someone trying to sell you a car based on what colour it is. What about its value?

We should be making informed fashion choices every day, as clothing is a ghastly environmental polluter. According to *Business Insider*, the fashion industry emits more carbon than international flights and maritime shipping combined.[45] Fashion production has more than doubled since 2000. We're cycling through clothing items more frequently, meaning we're purchasing more, not to mention that a vast majority of clothing ends up in the dump, hence fashion being a major carbon emissions culprit. It seems that we hem and haw more about making sure we invest in a hard-working $20 mascara than we do when faced with spending four to five figures on a dress. That mascara better be worth it, but we don't talk about the value of a wedding dress or if it is worthy of its price tag.

You're thinking, right, that's all fine and well, but there aren't many other places to look for dresses. Actually, there is, and we'll get to that. But if you've shopped around at some bridal boutiques and have fallen in love with a dress at one of them, do some digging to see what other retailers carry it (stores and online) and whether you can find it at a better price. Having alterations made by a tailor rather than the store might save some money, too.

LOOKING FOR BRIDAL SHOP ALTERNATIVES

There are lots of other places you can shop for gowns outside of the mainstay bridal boutiques. You can look out for end-of-year sales, vintage gowns, designer sample sales, consignment and resale stores, and more.

Loving Pre-Loved Gowns and Outfits

Do not write off a gown because another bride wore it for like, six hours. Seriously. There is something so progressive and responsible about resale bridal gowns. Would you buy a pair of jeans off-the-rack? Imagine how many people have tried on that pair. Now a previously loved dress doesn't seem so ridiculous, does it? If you explore this route, you might be able to afford an incredibly luxurious fabric that you may not otherwise be able to splurge on. And once that dress is properly fitted to your body, it will look like a new gown, anyway.

Understanding the New Bridal Frontier of Retail Stores and Rental Companies

All of a sudden, brands like Aritzia, Anthropologie, Reformation, and more have started to make simple and chic attire for wedding parties and brides alike. Smaller boutique shops started popping up, stocking their racks with beautiful and unique dresses that didn't cost a small fortune. Smaller boutiques are often nimbler, too, so brides don't have to wait the typical timelines of larger stores. Clothing rental companies can also be major scores, too. Check out Rent the Runway, Poshare, Lending Luxury, and RentmyDress.com.

This turn of fortune has allowed for brides to take back their sense of style in a fresh new way. No longer are we beholden to a look that simply isn't doing us any favours and that also doesn't actually "feel" like us.

Appreciating the Local Designer

One other route, which we cannot recommend enough, is to support a local designer. You'll get to know a local designer in your area who can tell you the story behind your gown. What inspired the design? How did they select the fabric? That particular shade? They can also tailor that dress with an extra touch because they made it. They know exactly how to make the neckline sit just so or get the back to hide your bra line ever-so-perfectly. You'll appreciate that dress — no, you'll love that dress — just a little bit more. We're also here for supporting local designers because you'll likely walk away with a more unique dress than had you shopped at a major chain retailer. Plus: what's more romantic than supporting a local artisan?

Dipping into Virtual Shopping

Online shopping for clothing can be stressful, chaotic, and nerve-racking at the best of times. With no consistent sizing across the board, finding something that is a perfect fit is a shot in the dark. Not to mention seeing how a dress or piece will drape and how the fabric will move. This is where your sleuthing skills will come in handy. Buying wedding attire online will require some work, but, yes, it can be worth it — having the internet at your fingers tips means that you literally have an unlimited supply of options. There are frocks and accessories aplenty from stores like the aforementioned Aritzia, Reformation, and Anthropologie, and a myriad of other smaller boutiques that often carry more pared down but still incredibly chic and stylish attire. You can also look to Net-A-Porter or Shopbop or SSENSE for contemporary, fashion-forward dresses, suiting, etc., that are not necessarily bridal. We're all about you feeling like yourself on your wedding day, whatever that entails.

The rise of shopping online for bridalwear has been slower than for most other clothing categories, and that tracks because purchasing something for your "big day" has been fraught with incredibly high expectations and an immense amount of pressure. And, as you may have guessed, we're here to tell you that it doesn't have to be that way.

Look to online shopping as an option in your overall outfit experience, but know that it doesn't quite end when you press purchase. As Indian fashion designer Sabyasachi Mukherjee told journalist Praachi Raniwala for a *New York Times* piece called "A Less Lavish Look for India's Wedding Industry" in July 2020, e-commerce is playing an even bigger role in the luxury bridal arena, but as complementary to the sector, not a replacement. And this applies not just to the luxury market.

You will need to do some work to make an online purchase work for you. The best way to prepare for an online shopping adventure is to grab a vinyl measuring tape (you can find one at Walmart, Michael's, or Amazon) and have your precise measurements at the ready before you type in those credit card numbers and press click to buy. You may need to grab a pal to help you out here. Record everything you can, from chest to waist to hips and even your height. Funnily enough, the old carpenter's rule of measuring twice also applies to clothing measurements. Luckily there are YouTube videos that can help you out when it comes to measuring everything properly. And all this is important because a U.K. 8 and a U.S. 8 vary greatly. Thankfully, most websites will provide detailed measurements for each piece they are selling.

Depending on how the look fits, you may need to size up — and this is where the in-store or in-person part takes centre stage. A seamstress or tailor will be your new best friend. If the dress is looser and more relaxed, stay true to size, because if there is anything out of sync with your figure, you can still have it altered to fit more snuggly. If you're looking for something that is more form-fitting, it might be best to go up one size. This will ensure that there is enough room to take things in at the hips or bust if either area needs some attention. Both of these tips will ensure that you look incredible in your off-the-rack piece that has now been tailor-made to fit you.

Other things you should take into consideration:

Know where you're buying from. Research the online vendor before you click buy, see if they have any reviews, and see how they interact with customers through their social-media accounts. This research includes knowing what their return policy is. You don't want to buy something only to realize that you cannot return it for a full refund if it isn't what you want to wear on your wedding day.

Don't be afraid to ask questions. Some sites have online concierges to help with any questions, like how is the fit, where is the piece manufactured, etc. If there is no such concierge, send an email. If you have q's about the colour, ask for a fabric swatch. And if they don't provide the measurements, here's where you can ask.

Do your purchasing well in advance. If you're being super spontaneous and getting married in a month, your options may be a bit more limited (stick to a retailer you already know, perhaps?), but if you can, give yourself four to six months, especially if the vendor is from outside your country and/or continent. This should give you loads of time for manufacturing, shipping, and tailoring.

Save yourself from credit card fraud. (Seriously, you don't have time to worry about that right now!) Make sure that you're using a secured site. The S in https:// stands for *secure*. Or you can check to see if a reputable e-commerce software company handles their transactions, like Shopify, etc.

Knowing Thy Dress

Don't buy your dress until you have asked the following:

- Who is doing the alterations and how much will they cost? You want no surprises, like having to travel a half hour to a freelance seamstress that the bridal boutique outsources to or the cost for alterations being double what you expect.

- How many fittings you will have and how close to your wedding the last fitting will be? Pro tip: if they are charging you per each fitting, you can try to skip one. The fitting closest to your wedding is the one that matters the most, anyway.
- What undergarments can/can't I wear with this? If you hate going braless, find this out now, not after you've committed to a dress. Plan on bringing your undergarments to your fittings.
- Can I find this dress at a better price elsewhere? Have you combed other boutiques, online, or tried to find it preloved?
- Is there a trunk show coming up from the designer? Trunk shows normally offer a discount for gowns sold, so you could save 15 percent and meet the designer, who may give you some ideas for how to style it.
- Will this dress be ready by my wedding date? Never make assumptions about how long it will take for your dress to arrive once it has been ordered.
- Is the sample for sale? If the sample for your dress is for sale and in good condition, it can be a great way to save some money.
- How many liberties can I take with customizing the dress? Some dresses are pretty fixed and can't be altered too far beyond their original design. If your wishes go beyond what this dress can be transformed into, it isn't the dress for you.
- What shape will my gown be in when I pick it up? Will it be steamed and packed in a box? Will you get to check it out while you're still in the store? Ask how to store it at home or for transportation advice if your gown needs to go on a plane.
- Can I get in and out of this dress or is major assistance required? The staff might have some advice for the hidden zipper or getting the bustle just so. Don't be shy about asking for their advice.
- Is it missing anything? Are the buttons and zipper all working? Seams all looking top notch? Inspect it.

GETTING TO KNOW SUITS

If you dreamed of your wedding dress your whole life, cool. If you didn't, also cool. There's no one way to be a bride.

For those less interested in a dress and feeling a suit or tuxedo, times are also changing. Many of us can remember guys in high school renting their tuxedo for prom. Dresses were bought and tuxes were rented. Thank goodness, economically and sartorially, there are better options for everyone that steer clear of ill-cut suits.

Suits are more practical than wedding dresses. Let's get real: the odds of a wedding dress being repurposed are pretty slim. But a classic, well-made suit that you wear on your wedding day can absolutely be a staple in your closet. A dark charcoal grey or midnight blue suit will look just as gorgeous at your wedding as it will (with a different tie, shirt, and shoes) at work (or job interviews or your friend's wedding).

A suit is an investment that's far, far more practical than a wedding dress. Harvey James, contributor to *British GQ*, agrees that the old tropes still exist, that weddings are women's business,[46] but men are feeling increased pressure to look good that day. "There is definitely more pressure to look better than before. With the explosion of social media making weddings much more documented and publicized, I think that weighs on the decisions that grooms will make. And also, to try to get all of their mates looking as good as possible, too, is all part of eliciting jealousy and one-upmanship, that signifies social-media competitiveness."

He points to the increasing access to cheaper materials that gives men more options for suiting. He's seeing more relaxed tailoring, more toward the upper end of smart-casual, lighter materials, and lighter shades of suits becoming normal for wedding-goers. As for the groom and the groomsmen, "That remains fairly rigidly traditional, because if you can't wear tails to your own wedding, when can you wear them?" Good point.

"I think most of all, they're looking for something that is formal and makes a suave, stylish statement. Some want to really revel in the tradition and formality of it and will go tails, or black tie. Others will just want something that looks half decent on." What everyone should plan on, James recommends, is getting it tailored properly by a professional and going for something a little more robust and of higher quality so it can be worn ad infinitum. Second-hand suits are not to be passed up, either. "I've seen some cracking preowned suits recently," says James. Get it tailored and ensure it is still in top-notch condition.

Rented tuxes are still a thing, particularly for those who want everyone in the wedding party to match.

ORGANIZING THE REST OF THE OUTFIT

In the spirit of you doing you — which applies to the whole wedding and is obviously the mantra of this book, but your bridal look especially — don't feel sucked into buying accessories, makeup, beauty treatments, or other stuff just because you're a bride. We're all for treating ourselves to some solid self-care, but we're not for the bridal vortex. And some of the trappings that accompany The Dress are pretty loaded. If you're going for the whole bridal shebang, don't let us stop you, but you should know where those things come from.

Wanting to Veil ... or Not

Feeling pressure to wear a veil because it is part of the usual bridal ensemble? Consider this: The root of bridal veils isn't very romantic at all.

The Romans worried that brides could be enchanted by evil spirits, so they covered a bride in veils (often full length and flame coloured)[47] to protect her. What's more of a buzzkill is that, historically, many brides were veiled and the first time her betrothed would see her face was when he lifted her veil. The reason was so that he couldn't pull the chute on the bride if he didn't like what he saw.[48]

The veil is also a nod to that aforementioned snobbery. Even though Queen Victoria popularized the white wedding gown in the mid-18th century, veils were popular well before that. A symbol of modesty and innocence, the veil has been a fixture in religious ceremonies around the world, from Christianity to Judaism to Islam. During Victorian times, when a lot of these "modern" wedding customs were galvanized, the grandeur of the veil was a sign of the bride's status. The more important the bride, the longer the veil and train. Lastly, the act of her father "giving away" the bride to her new husband was quite literal. The transaction was complete when the husband lifted her veil.

All that said, adding a veil to your ensemble really depends on the look you're going for, what feels right for you, and whether you have room in your budget (they are an added expense, after all).

Veils range in length and material, and therefore price. If you're feeling princess vibes, you could always go for a 16-foot long silk embroidered veil, à la Meghan Markle when she wed Prince Harry in 2018. Said veil reportedly took longer to make than the actual dress, and likely came with a pretty hefty price tag. (If you're marrying a prince of England, you better go all out!)

How much room do you need for this accoutrement in your overall budget? It all depends on the length and fabrication that you want. There are versions that fall just below the shoulders that can start around $100 (CDN). Or if you want to go OTT regal, a floor-length veil can cost upward of $500 (CDN). Then you also have to factor in material. Simple tulle veils, which can look incredibly chic, can start around $60 (CDN) (again depending on length). If you're looking for beading or embroidery, you're likely looking at spending $100 (CDN) plus. The nice thing about getting embroidered is you can add some extra-special elements to the design. Angelina Jolie added doodles from her children onto her veil when she married Brad Pitt in 2014. Charlotte Alter's article "Here's How Much It Costs to Get Your Veil Embroidered Like Angelina's" in *Time* magazine estimated this personal touch cost the couple around $3,500 (USD), because of how intricate all the drawings were. Going custom will always cost more than off-the-rack, and you can still find some lovely options in store or online. Crafty sites like Etsy host a plethora of artisans, so that could be a great place to start if you're working within a budget. Otherwise, have at it — make your veil as personal as you want, if you want.

Lusting for the Bouquet

When else have you ever walked around with a bouquet of flowers? Ever? They are a good fix if you're a fidgety person, but it's a little weird, isn't it? Clutching an artfully constructed handful of flowers?

Way back when, in medieval times, people bathed very infrequently, sometimes only once a year. The most popular time was in the spring, which is also why June was historically a popular month for weddings.[49] You'd be so fresh and sexy walking down that aisle, having bathed three weeks ago. Back then, brides still wanted to smell sexy, so they'd carry a bouquet of flowers to cover up their body odour and also to bring them good luck. The plague also helped seal the custom, as people would often clutch little bouquets of dill and garlic, as they were thought to have medicinal properties.[50]

The Victorians took the custom to a new level when they got into the whole business of the language of flowers — which some couples still look to today. It's pretty lovely and romantic if you can look past its body-odour-and-plague-covering roots. Stephanotis meant marital bliss,[51] baby's breath innocence, chrysanthemums wealth and abundance, gardenias purity,[52] and so on.

Rejecting the Garter

Steel yourself up for the backstory on this, it is a bit creepy. Ever heard of the game "finger the stocking"? That's where the old garter comes from. Back in medieval England, people were pretty obsessed with their heirs. The patriarchy, always on its bullshit. They were so obsessed with a bride conceiving an heir that after the ceremony, all the wedding guests would actually pop into the wedding chamber to inspect the bride's undergarments for signs that the bride and groom had consummated the marriage.[53] They'd finger her stockings, to be exact. It (by which we mean the signs of the bride losing her virginity) was an assurance that the couple was getting down to the business of procreating, but it also helped legitimize the wedding. A marriage was more likely to be legally recognized if it was consummated.

If you've been to a wedding where a garter is being awkwardly taken off a bride's leg and she is trying to look like she's cool with it, but her face says otherwise, it's been that way for a long, long time.

Yearning for the Right Shoes, Shoes, Shoes

Shoes can either be the sassy centrepiece of your wedding day ensemble or they can be well hidden under any floor-length gown. Either way, comfort is always key when it comes to choosing footwear. (Sorry, we're over the whole suffering for fashion thing.) You'll be standing in these babies for hours on end, posing for photos, walking around greeting guests, you know the rest.

If the shoes are your showstopper, there are a few things to consider. Make sure they're broken in and that you've worn them (in or out of the house) for longer than an hour. You don't want to deal with blisters or any sort of pain on the day of your wedding. Speaking of blisters, adding blister tape to any tender areas as a backup is of the utmost importance! And having gel insoles, if possible, will also help to turn down any pain.

Or you can forego this entire hullabaloo, make like Man Repeller's Leandra Medine, and sport a pair of kicks under your gown. Medine's were of the platform variety, to add some height to her teeny tiny frame, but we can bet she was incredibly comfortable for the entire day. Keds and Kate Spade paired up for a collection of bridal sneakers, and there's even a wedding sneakers section on etsy.com. Girl, you've got options.

GROOVING ON YOUR ATTENDANTS' ATTIRE

Get ready for more weirdness. Remember how ancient Romans put a *Hunger Games*–esque veil on brides to protect her from evil spirits? Well, those Romans were also sticklers for RSVPing. In order for a wedding to be legally binding, it required 10 witnesses.[54] Many think

THESE HIGH HEEL-WEARING
TIPS REALLY WORK

1. Take an anti-inflammatory prior to stepping into your shoes. Taking an Aleve or even CBD can help keep painful steps at bay. Celebs like Olivia Wilde, Busy Phillips, and shoe designer Tamara Mellon all swear by massaging a CBD lotion into their feet prior to heading out to major events in major heels.
2. This one comes osteopath approved: Tape your third and fourth toes together on each foot, which is a method of taking the pressure off the balls of your feet.
3. If you're rocking six-inch stilettos or higher for your wedding, snag a pair of three- to four-inch heels for the dancing portion of the evening. You'll still look sophisticated and you'll have taken some of the pressure off, literally.

that this laid the foundation for the modern wedding party, which the Victorians solidified.

Historically, bridesmaids served a larger purpose than witnessing the wedding: They also served as lookalikes. Bridesmaids all had to dress like the bride to confuse evil spirits.[55] Talk about taking one for the team. So quit bitching if you've ever had to don a fuchsia taffeta frock — bridesmaids back then were ready to get possessed by evil spirits so the bride could have a really nice wedding day.

There's even more to this. Brides would sometimes get kidnapped! People would be waiting to steal her and the fancy dowry that came with her. Having a bunch of bridesmaids as bridal decoys greatly reduced the risk of the actual bride being stolen.[56] In Rome and feudal China, bridesmaids were red herrings in case someone else wanted to marry the bride, or she was stolen back by her family. WT actual F. Not to put too fine of a point on it, but let's not forget the sisters that got hitched before us: that was a straight-up financial transaction.

And we'd be remiss if we didn't drop something about modern-day bridesmaid here. Your squad. Your team. Your BFFs. For all the fuckery that goes into having a wedding party (anyone obsessed with weddings has seen horror stories online about fights between bridesmaids causing major friction, and sometimes eviction from the party all together!), this can be a time to bond even more with your best friends. After all, they have your back, which is why you want them there in their full glory on your wedding day. The most important part of this arrangement is, of course, what those friends will wear.

We say out with taffeta and pre-programmed wedding parties where every person wears a version of the same look. For every teal, blue, or purple wedding party, we've seen white-on-white, floral frocks aplenty, and an ombré of similarly hued outfits taking over wedding feeds. And we're here for it. Giving your friends some creative licence, within your framework, of course, will help them feel like themselves and will not put any constraints on price or fit. Consider yourself the creative director here, not a wedding dictator. It will save face with your friends and can truly create some beautiful pictures and memories with your crew.

Real-Life Wedding Stories

Cody works in fashion editorial and Turner in the beauty industry. Turner and Cody met on Tinder the first day Turner downloaded the app. They liked each other instantly and thus began their romance.

They got engaged on New Year's Eve 2017, and within seven months had a spectacular wedding on top of a mountain at the Alta Lakes in Colorado. The wedding was anything but turnkey (they handwrote and wrapped every single invitation, with a feather and sprig of eucalyptus included).

They invited 50 guests for an intimate ceremony, down a dirt road and through a ghost town, just their guests and the jaw-dropping scenery: not a single embellishment, aside from the handmade benches that Turner's family built and brought from Wyoming.

The reception for 250 guests was on a remote ranch. Despite the secluded location, it is worth noting that they still managed to get noise complaints. The police were called to rein in the party.

"We had this incredible farm-to-table menu served family style, and an unwavering commitment to a green, sustainable wedding. There were no plastics whatsoever," says Cody. Every element of the wedding, while it took time and energy, was a reflection of them as individuals and as a couple. Was it easy? No. Was it worth it? Totally.

They started from scratch, because they didn't see themselves reflected in any wedding planning materials. Cody explains it was difficult, particularly in the early stages of their planning. "Being gay and based in Utah is difficult to navigate. It was hard. There is not a lot for same-sex couples. We didn't have those resources to plan something that felt like us." They ended up finding a book for gay grooms called *Getting Groomed*, and while it wasn't perfect, it was something. The couple soon found their footing and started bringing things to life.

Turner says that having the right wedding planner was key. "We found this incredible planner that had done a few weddings in rural Colorado, some of which were same-sex couples. She really helped refine our ideas and keep us focused." What's more, having a wedding planner that had worked with same-sex couples gave them confidence that she would work with vendors that would value and respect them. "We knew she'd hire the right vendors," adds Turner. Cody, having lived in Los Angeles and New York, doesn't take that for granted. "Things are different on the coasts, so much so that it is easy to forget what's happening in the middle of the country. It is a scary feeling."

Growing up in Utah, Turner explains that much of the wedding discourse didn't apply to gay couples. "The wedding culture here is such that we weren't seen. It was tricky to get my brain out of the traditional temple wedding. A bit of it was triggering for me. There felt like countless options of sleeved dresses for Mormon brides, but nothing for us. I felt lost along the way."

Still, they found ways to authentically represent their cultures. For Cody, that was a Native American ceremony and symbolism, for Turner, it was prayer. Their own cultural enmeshment was furthered by their guests, with a range of races, religions, and backgrounds, coming together to celebrate their love. Their attire was also carefully selected. They found a local clothier to make custom suits, with both men choosing bespoke touches, down to their buttons. Both wore white. Turner chose a western-inspired three-piece suit; Cody chose a white floral shirt under his suit, as a nod to his Indigenous roots.

They rented a huge house to stay with their wedding attendants before the wedding, who all brought various talents. They stayed up late into the night putting together flower arrangements. "We didn't want anyone to feel like they were working, but we did want to bring our friends along for the journey in ways that felt meaningful," says Cody.

Cody's auntie braided his hair with an eagle feather tucked into his tresses. Turner wore a cream cowboy hat. They had 18 attendants, men and women, representing a range of ages. Cody's cousin played a drum and sang as they walked down the aisle. Before exchanging vows, Cody's grandfather performed a smudging ceremony. (Miraculously, at this point in the ceremony, an eagle swooped down to pluck a fish out of the lake. Magic, right?) A close friend, who came in from the Bay area for the occasion, married them. Even their four-legged friends were represented. The couple's two dogs (Guillermo, a French bulldog/pug mix, and Bixby the Boston terrier) were in attendance, and each had a signature cocktail served in their honour (a whiskey sour named the Bixby Sour and a margarita named Guillermorita).

Looking back, the couple admits it was easy to feel pulled away from their vision. "As we were getting our plans off the ground, it became very clear that we had to stay true to who we are. We didn't want to lose ourselves in the wedding industry because of things that we were 'supposed' to do, or that we've been taught that we have to do. We did spend a lot of time on the details, but we really wanted our wedding to be a reflection of us and our love."

Turner cautions how easy it is for couples to chase trends. "It was so difficult to find ways of acknowledging our cultures without appropriating or being tokenistic. Some elements of Cody's culture, like feathers and teepees, are sort of hipster cool right now. We're very aware that the wedding industry pulls in elements of various cultures and tries to make money off them."

When it came to deciding what their new last name should be, their choice was unexpected but something emblematic of their hopes for the future. AhTave means "new day" in Ute. "We chose this name to reclaim and pay homage to my family's language and culture. Both of us have had personal battles with our last names and felt that by choosing to go with this family name we were honouring both the present, past, and future."

5 Picture-Perfect Couple
You *Can* Avoid the Pressure to Look Perfect

The apotheosis of the bridal industry is its collective obsession with how brides look. Apparently we're not only okay with this, we're also willing to shell out big bucks to go along. It isn't enough to wear makeup; you'd better buy all new makeup and hire a professional makeup artist to refine your look. It isn't enough to style your hair; you'd better invest in salon conditioning treatments for a year in advance then book several trials to find the perfect stylist. It isn't enough to take good care of your skin; you'd better go for quarterly chemical peels and get a pop of Botox before the wedding.

Sara, a recent bride, felt like a spectacle.[57] "I love speaking in front of crowds professionally, but this felt different: I felt very much on display. I get dressed up for occasions, but as a bride, people were more effusive with their compliments, like 'Wow, you look so gorgeous'. The subtext was that some sort of transformation or metamorphosis had taken place."

Policing women's bodies and holding women to outrageous standards is nothing new, but when did things get so out of control? Chalk it up to celebrity culture, the editorialization of weddings, and social media, which put a magnifying glass on perfection.

GIVING THE BOOT TO BRIDAL BOOTCAMPS

Grab a barf bag then google "bridal bootcamp." It is ridiculous. Cleanses, diets, bridal workouts, training "trouble areas" of the body — the list seems endless. The idea of #SheddingForTheWedding is practically synonymous with getting engaged. "Even though a bride may feel she is drowning in all the planning involved in a wedding," advises one bridal website, "it will be very advantageous to also [create a detailed] weight-loss strategy."[58] According to a Cornell University study, more than 70 percent of engaged women were planning to lose weight.[59] An Australian study[60] followed almost 350 brides for six months after their weddings. Half expressed a desire to lose weight before the wedding and nearly a third were advised to lose weight by someone. Another study in Australia found that the majority of brides in both the U.S. and Australia aimed to lose around 20 pounds prior to the wedding.[61]

Kristen, a Toronto fitness trainer with a past that includes disordered eating, was downright offended. "It makes me furious that there is this pressure on brides to lose weight for one single day, for a matter of hours," she laments. "I had this panic. What if I gained a bit of weight and wouldn't be 'perfect'? Whatever that means. All my history of disordered eating and body-image issues came flooding back because of the societal pressure to look like a cake topper. When you make those sorts of demands on the body, it makes you angry and bitchy. You're starving. And for what, a few hours?" Kristen won't take on a client wanting help to lose weight for their wedding. "I will never teach a bridal bootcamp. Ever. There's no place for pain or punishment. Health and fitness are a lifestyle, not a goal for one day."

One recently wed woman found Instagram and Pinterest to be dark holes that started making her feel pretty bad, pretty quickly.[62] "The year we got married, we were surrounded by other weddings, so it is hard not to compare. There was pressure to be very image conscious in a way that I had never been my entire life." She had never worried about her weight, and yet as the wedding approached, "I went on a diet and the gym turned into a stressor rather than a stress release. If I didn't go to the gym, I'd feel guilty. I was never the type to fantasize about my wedding, then I started following these accounts on social media, then ended up down the rabbit hole, facing this deep pressure to be and look a certain way. Then that tacit low-grade pressure from social media starts to turn into pressure among friend groups, this sort of woman-on-woman pressure." She talked to her husband, but she could tell that he didn't *really* get it. "The pressure was very real. When the wedding industry is encouraging women to be your best self, what it is really saying is *look* your best self. I got the stuff to make my eyelashes grow, worked out constantly, dieting for the first time in my entire life. I look back and I like how the photos look but to be honest, if I hadn't done a thing I'd probably look almost the same, but I'll never get the time or emotional energy back that I lost for those six months."

Dr. Sara Santarossa has devoted much of her career to health promotion and health education around body image and self-esteem. Her research explores how social media impacts body image, and the role of media literacy. Interestingly, she recently got married. "I'm immersed in such a body-positive world, so I was very aware of the pressure on my bridesmaids," who ranged in sizes from 2 to 18. "Because of what I do professionally, I find people are typically pretty sensitive to what they say around me. Once I was getting married, it was like a free-for-all and people talked about wanting to lose weight as if it were a given. When it came to people who know me, they know what I'm about, they started talking about their own bodies in a way that just stunned me. I didn't know what to do with it. I really just wanted people to feel good about themselves. I most certainly didn't want people to be hard on their bodies on account of my wedding."[63]

Shit got even more real for Dr. Santarossa when she was shopping for her own wedding dress. She recalls trying on dresses and a sales associate commented on her arms and back looking a little too muscular, insinuating that she had overdone it by trying to get fit for her wedding. "I was like, 'No, I'm active.' It is courageous to have my voice when people were saying things about my arms."

Her research has shown that appearance-based comments online can have a detrimental effect on body confidence. "You see a bride post a photo and the comments are like 'you're so beautiful,' 'you look gorgeous' … if you're only giving appearance-based comments, you're competing with yourself to get *more* of that same feedback." What a powerful insight. Why don't we tell couples in general (and brides in particular) that they look happy? Dr. Santarossa confides that the best comment she got was from someone at her bridal shower. "A woman I know from the Bulimia Anorexia Nervosa Association said to me, 'You know, you really look like yourself.'"

Appreciating the Skin You're In

Unfortunately, things go deeper than weight, and brides are inundated with messages to not only look thin, but also to look perfect. One study reported that close to 40 percent of brides intended to tan in preparation for their wedding.[64] Some people slather themselves in chemicals to get a bronzed look. Some get it by baking in the sun or a tanning bed. Others risk their health by trying to make their skin as fair as possible. A study of a Somali community in Minnesota reported that women used skin-lightening cream more than usual leading up to a wedding.[65]

Fatima Lodhi is a diversity activist and founder of Dark is Divine, a global anti-colourism campaign. Based in Pakistan, she shares that in South Asia everyone is trying to have the fairest skin, the lighter the better. "The way dark skin is portrayed to sell products is horrible. It is treated as a disease that needs to be corrected." At Lodhi's own wedding, there were two celebrations, as she and her husband are from different cities. "When I went to his city to have the wedding, I booked an appointment at a local beauty salon to get ready. They didn't have a foundation or powder to match my skin tone. They had to use a contouring kit. I looked so cakey, so white, I was not happy at all."[66] This is, unfortunately, standard. "Brides come in to get their makeup done and leave the beauty salon looking [like they have] a different skin tone. They look white." The message for brides and grooms is that fairer skin is more attractive.

Sadly, it runs much deeper than makeup. Lodhi explains that skin lightening also intersects with class. "You see everyone bleaching their skin. It is cheap, you can get a bleach for 100 rupees." Mercury has been found in some lightening creams and soaps, according to the World Health Organization. Mercury suppresses the production of melanin in the body, but it can also damage the kidneys and brain when absorbed through the skin, and it accumulates in the body. Other skin-lightening methods include chemical peels, which remove the top layer of skin, leaving it more exposed to harmful rays and pollutants. Laser treatments are an even more aggressive approach that break up the skin's pigmentation, sometimes with permanently damaging results.

In talking to Lodhi, it became clear that whether a bride lives in Toronto, New York, London, or Islamabad, she is inundated with messages that her appearance is something to improve and correct. "The industry is selling it, and we're buying it. It hits the nail right on our emotions, and we buy it. We let this happen. There is an industry doing this for money, to make women feel awful about how they look." Lodhi understands how very slippery the slope is. "Girls have this fantasy of getting married and looking beautiful … I don't blame them, but we have to find the willpower to push against this."

PUTTING PRESSURE ON THE GUYS

The industry is chipping away at men's self-esteem, too. The pressure for men to lose weight before their weddings isn't as well documented as it is in women, but that doesn't mean it doesn't exist. Men's health magazines preach diets to slim down fast to get "wedding ready." Pre-wedding "brotox" is now a thing, with men going for injectables to give the appearance of a more chiselled jawline or soften crow's feet. Some grooms are splurging for hair transplants. An entire vernacular has emerged to pressure men to be as vain as women as their wedding approaches. In addition to brotox, there is xeoman, a take on Xeomin (a botulinum injection similar to Botox), and a manlycure, the dude version of a manicure. There are also the popular guybrows, the plucking, waxing, tinting, and what-have-you for picture-perfect eyebrows.

Groom Nando Rodriguez shared his experience of losing weight before his wedding.[67] He intentionally bought a blazer a few sizes too small, committed to it fitting perfectly for his wedding. It was a splurge purchase and going to have to work. Rodriguez said he turned to extreme juicing. "I still ate food," he said, "but I just made sure to have a green juice in the morning, a green juice at lunch, and ate pretty limited at dinner." He followed the juice plan for three months and, unsurprisingly, "it was not a happy situation." Rodriguez said the diet plan was particularly challenging because he was stressed at work, and his partner wasn't following the same extreme plan. His partner tried doing the juice diet, too, "But he'd sneak out and eat bread or something." Rodriguez said his partner had never once commented on his weight, but that he was supportive of his desire to shed some pounds. "He'd eat in the bedroom with the door closed so I couldn't smell the food."

GOING TO EXTREMES

Psychology Today reported that almost half of brides-to-be recruited from a wedding expo (46%) were targeting an ideal wedding weight that was on average 20 pounds less than their current weight.[68] Some women are willing to go to extreme measures to lose weight before their wedding. Some crash diet, some starve themselves, or some work out obsessively. Others stick a feeding tube down their nose. That's right. A woman spent eight days on a feeding tube, which cost a whopping $1,500 (USD) for 10 days, to fit into her dress.[69] She explained, "I don't have all of the time on the planet just to focus an hour and a half a day to exercise, so I came to the doctor, I saw the diet, and I said, 'You know what? Why not? Let me try it.' So I decided to go ahead and give it a shot."

ADJUSTING YOUR EXPECTATIONS

Images of perfection drive women into bootcamp classes, tanning beds, skin whitening, plastic surgeons' offices, and the aesthetician's chair to apply those false lashes just so. What was wrong with the woman before she had all these things done to her? Absolutely nothing. There's nothing to correct before your wedding, except maybe your expectations.

"The wedding industry upsells to all of us, and now we're selling it to each other through social media. The bridesmaid trip with white bikinis and rosé all day is a new phenomenon that is setting a difficult standard," believes Alison Slight, an event designer in Toronto. "I'm unsure why couples are following this template, as it is increasingly unoriginal and puts a lot of pressure on those involved both financially and in terms of the level of commitment and time you are asking for. It is sometimes good to step back. You have the ability to do something different."

Bailey Parnell is founder and researcher at #SafeSocial, an organization that helps people gain the benefits of social media with fewer of the risks. She examines the myriad ways that social media affects our sense of self — the greatest of which she believes to be social comparisons.[70] "Social-comparison theory is essentially the idea that people compare themselves as a means of self-evaluating to understand and construct their identity. This is a very normal part of the human experience long before social media," she explains. For example, in real life, a comparison could simply be that you know you are tall because you look around and see that everyone else is shorter than you. That helps to create your identity as a tall person. When it comes to constructing our self-image, we also compare ourselves in more loaded areas such as appearance, wealth, opinions, career, skills, abilities, and more.

Another important aspect of social-comparison theory is that the more similar you are to whom you're comparing yourself, the stronger the comparison will be. Ahem, brides following other brides. Finally, comparison is also directional, in that it can be upward (looking up to someone and seeing yourself as worse off), neutral (seeing yourself as equal), or downward (looking down on someone or seeing yourself as better off). Parnell cautions that continuous upward comparison to people like you is the worst-case scenario for mental health and self-image, "Because you are constantly looking down on yourself in a way."

What's the harm though? Well, when we apply social-comparison theory to the social-media world, it can be a recipe for disaster. "Many people follow people like them or whom they want to be like. Those people are only posting their highlight reels of the best and brightest moments of their lives. Now you can compare all the time, it is quantified for everyone to see, and it is often upward in direction. This affects our self-image in almost every aspect of our lives."

One particular area that Parnell explores is social media and women's bodies, the ideal being thin with a small waist and not much body fat. "Body image and appearance was the area in which my participants compared themselves most offline and online. In addition, when they compared themselves on Instagram, the comparisons were more frequent and more upward in direction, which can lead to feelings of our own bodies not measuring up to the ideals online.

"Social media is often quite literally unreal. People manipulate and edit their photos (beyond recognition sometimes) trying to make their ideal unreal seem real." This means we may often be comparing ourselves to bodies/lives/weddings/showers/parties that are ACTUALLY NOT REAL. "How can anyone compare digitally with manipulated skin or teeth?" quips Parnell. "We can't."

Of course, social media isn't to blame for women feeling shitty about our bodies. That predates social media. One hopeful point that Parnell relays is that there is more body positivity messaging and accounts on social media than there ever was in traditional media. "Instead of saying, 'Get off social media to feel better about your body,' I instead encourage following people that make you feel strong and better about who you are."

The over-the-topness of weddings has created a pressure to plan them for how *we want people* to perceive us, rather than get deep and introspective about what we actually want. There is an outward focus on how we want to be perceived. When it comes to understanding ourselves, social interaction plays a huge role. This is American sociologist Charles Horton Cooley's theory of the looking glass. We make decisions based on the image we want to project.

OBSERVING THE CONFLUENCE OF CELEBRITY AND SOCIAL MEDIA

"I think that wedding obsession and then the rise in our obsession with celebrity weddings happened concurrently," Elaine Lui, aka LaineyGossip, the powerhouse celebrity columnist and television personality, told Michelle when they spoke in April 2020.[71]

One of the first celebrity weddings was the royal nuptials of Princess Diana and Charles, Prince of Wales, in 1981. This was *an event.* Not unlike every royal wedding since, people set their alarms for awful o'clock to watch it live and fawned over the pomp: the huge wedding, the grand procession, the massive dress with those unforgettable sleeves. It was a real-life fairy-tale wedding and once we saw it, we couldn't get enough. The 1980s was when every part of the Western white wedding started to get big: guest lists, bridal parties, gowns, and hair. Now, thanks to the internet and an obsession with celebrity culture, we see countless over-the-top glitzy weddings with endless bridal parties and wedding guests — and the endless budget to match. It normalizes extravagant weddings and all of their trappings.

The world seemed to binge on the weddings of real-life princesses of late, Kate Middleton and Meghan Markle. "You can't deny he is handsome," Lui says of Markle's now-husband Prince Harry. "He's funny. He's sporty. I mean he's right out of a YA novel. And then on top of that, his sometimes-dramatic past dating life. And then on top of that he ends up with a Hollywood actress. And on top of that their wedding was in the most fairy-tale setting, the quintessential English town at a castle with a carriage ride that was so charming because of the fact that it was in Windsor.

"Will and Kate's wedding was bananas, as well," continues Lui, who reported on both weddings for Canadian television. "But there is something to the carriage being drawn through a small town where the streets are very small. All of that combined made for, yes, one of the most intriguing weddings of recent history.

"I think for humanity there are really only a few main storylines," says Lui. "Love, hate, betrayal, suffering. And so love has a very powerful lure.… That performance of love is quite intoxicating for the observer. And, let's face it, celebrities are more often than not very attractive. These are very pretty people marrying other pretty people, and we like to look at pretty things."

What we don't see are endless budgets, sponsor kickbacks, heavily edited photos, and publishing deals. Justin Timberlake and Jessica Biel's wedding cost an estimated $6.5 million (USD). Kim Kardashian's wedding (her third) to Kanye West was estimated to cost $12 million (USD). These are obviously not wedding budgets in the grasp of us mere mortals, yet we see them constantly in magazines, on TV, and on social media, to the degree that they are oddly normalized.

Ironically, the very people who can afford to bankroll the most lavish of weddings often get their costs offset by brands that want the alignment and exposure. That's right: When you're rich and famous enough to afford to bankroll the most lavish of weddings, you get things comp'd.

When fashion influencer Chiara Ferragni married rapper Fedez (aka Federico Leonardo Lucia), every conceivable element of their wedding was #sponsored. Everything from the Alitalia flights to the custom Dior dresses Ferragni wore (two of them) over their wedding weekend was sponsored.

Priyanka Chopra Jonas and Nick Jonas also had some #sponsored content during their multi-day wedding in India. Social-media posts featured Amazon's wedding gift registry (sponsored), Tiffany & Co. (yes, sponsored), and Ralph Lauren (yup, sponsored). Forest Essentials, a high-end beauty company, got a shout-out from Chopra Jonas for creating "personalized luxury Ayurveda sets" to give to the newlywed's family and friends (mmhmm, sponsored) and Elit Vodka provided product for Jonas' bachelor party.

Hot Tip: Edit Your Social-Media Feed

While you're aimlessly scrolling through bridal shit, looking for ideas or hate-watching someone's proposal video, know that you are literally making your own hell. The more you follow, like, and consume, the more you are telling Instagram, "Please give me more of this!" You need to do a deep social-media audit. Unfollow like you've never unfollowed before. Your algorithm will quickly adapt and stop serving up that crap. Do yourself a favour, because it's so easy to get lost or feel like you need to fit a certain bridal image.

Josh Spiegel, creative director at NY-based Birch Event Design, says celebrity culture plays a role in the continual one-upmanship of weddings. "When it comes to events, everyone is upping their game. A celebrity's wedding can creep up and everyone's idea of a wedding suddenly shifts. Some no longer feel up to par, because the celebrity factor really pushes people."[72]

One recently wed woman attested to this influence. Early into her wedding planning, she followed a few accounts on Instagram, some of which were high-end Toronto and New York wedding planners. "They perpetuate this incredible over-the-topness, but it normalizes that extravagance to the degree that when you're scrolling, it is easy to think 'Oh, this is just what a wedding looks like.'"

FEELING PRETTY UGLY

A quick scroll through some wedding forums reveals some really ugly truths behind the quest for prettiness:

> I'm about 75 days away from my wedding now and I'm really feeling the pressure to somehow transform myself into this beautiful bride that everyone expects to see. Not just on the day but in photos after.... I keep worrying that I am not going to be slim enough, pretty enough or have the best hair on the day. I feel like everyone is expecting to see some beautiful bride come down the aisle, but it's just going to be me in a big dress. No matter how good the hair and makeup person turns out to be it's still going to be just me and I'm just not very pretty. [73]

> I am really worried about my teeth on my wedding day ... I don't want to look back at my photos and be disgusted by my mouth.

> I lost so much weight from stress before the wedding that my dress had to be altered significantly from when I originally bought it.

> I am getting married in 13 days and while I am really looking forward to marrying my fiancé I am terrified I won't look as groomed and perfect as you are supposed to on your wedding day. There is so much pressure from magazines and other people to have the perfect dress, figure, tan, teeth, jewellery and hair. [74]

> Oh god I'm totally feeling this pressure — it's the worst! Seriously the pressure is unreal. [75]

EDITORIALIZING THE WEDDING

Ella, an established editor at a fashion magazine, felt some serious expectations as a bride.[76] "There was this pressure around what I would wear, working where I do." She opted for a voluminous long-sleeve gown from New York-based designer Danielle Frankel, though the pressure didn't end there.

"I work in the fashion industry. I've been petite my whole life. I'm acutely aware of how body-image issues are perpetuated. I find weddings are a good icebreaker, so when I'd meet people at events and make small talk, I'd often chat about my wedding. I was at a media preview event and someone passed me some food and said, 'Don't worry, it fits the wedding diet.'"

Ella also has an inside perspective on the quest to look perfect. "It is all about the photos," she explains. Weddings have become editorialized, the bride as thin as a model and the hair and makeup on par with a magazine shoot. "The truth is, if someone doesn't have their makeup professionally done, it shows in the photos. You can tell. The bar has been raised."

The *New York Times* ran a story hawking different workouts to cater to different gown shapes. With not a hint of irony, it was titled, "The Perfect Workout for Your Wedding Dress Silhouette," including diet advice and a caution to avoid getting muscles that are too broad. The original article (it has since been edited) cautioned that while swimming can be a great workout, "It should be done in moderation, so that your back does not get too wide."[77]

Muscles on a woman? How unfeminine. BOO HISSSSS.

The article was shared on Twitter (it seems to have since been deleted) and was suitably lambasted. "As someone getting married in 6 weeks who is sick of people talking about my body as an object: do better," wrote one user on Twitter. "The story line of the thin bride is played out," said one commenter. Another tweet, incidentally from NYT opinion columnist Jennifer Weiner, shot back, "You can also buy a wedding dress that fits the body you have and makes you feel good. That's an option, too."

The *New Yorker* published a heater of a satire titled "Literally the Only Workout for Your Wedding-Dress Silhouette." It featured such sage advice as for those planning to wear a ball gown: "Only eat round foods during the 3.14 months before your big day, and make sure to sign up for the Daily Rotation."

Gold. Pure gold.

TURNING YOUR BACK ON THE IDEA OF PERFECTION

Why *do* we expect brides to look perfect?

Well, for one, we wholesale objectify brides. From the spectacle of walking down the aisle to the lifting of the veil, traditionally brides have been things we visually consume. What's even more concerning is that some brides are taking their friends down with them. Enter the whole bridesmaids group-weight-loss situation. There is an entire new crop of fitness classes and bootcamps intended for wedding parties. We've also heard of brides mandating what swimwear their bridal parties wear to avoid pre-wedding tan lines. We've heard of brides having Botox parties for their bridesmaids or sending out coupons for diet meal delivery services. Let us go on the record to say that all of this is like paper underwear. Just because it exists, doesn't mean it is a good idea. If you are even remotely considering asking someone to change their appearance to be part of your wedding, you'd better check yourself.

A well-meaning person (but, let's be honest, total asshole) might suggest you drop a few pounds before dress shopping, or to spring for eyelash extensions. You do you.

Looking Like Yourself

Of course you want to look great at your wedding. You'll have all this attention on you, photos that you'll look at for years (hell, even your grandkids might look at), so we get it: It is natural to be image conscious and want to look your best. But there is looking great and then there is trying to look like someone else. We're talking entirely new hair, the Botox, the fake lashes ... when you add these things up, do you look like yourself? We assume you're marrying someone who loves you just the way you are, and if you're not, it is time to sit down for a serious, serious talk.

We're all for being healthy, so do 10 bootcamps if that's your jam — just don't do them for the sake of being thin at your wedding. Ditto crash diets. Eat for your health, not some construct of how a bride should look. Establish healthy eating habits as a couple and learn to shop and prepare dishes that are delicious and nutrient-dense. Do some cardio together, too, if you're picking up what we're putting down.

Real-Life Wedding Stories

LM and B met 10 years ago and got engaged within a year of meeting.

"As a part of the LGBTQ community, plus growing up in very liberal-minded Quebec, weddings weren't on my mind. Over the years, I was single, in monogamous relationships, in polyamorous relationships, casually dating, and everything in between. Marriage was just not on my radar.

"When I met my husband, I knew. I just knew. Once we were engaged, we started to get a little pressure from friends and family to have this wedding, and it got complicated: We couldn't agree on a guest list and my now-husband is a chef, so making decisions about food and venue were impossible. So for nine years we just debated every possible way to get married.

"We finally agreed to get married on our 10th anniversary of meeting, come hell or high water. We imposed this deadline on ourselves because we knew that without a deadline, it would be another 10 years. Then, of course, life happened and that deadline sort of snuck up on us. On the night of our 10th anniversary of meeting, we didn't feel like doing much, but were like, come on, come on, let's go out. We went out and came home quite tipsy. Okay, maybe a little more than tipsy.

"We fired up the laptop and hosted our own impromptu wedding on the spot, live streamed from our apartment for our Facebook friends. We twisted up some newspaper to make rings, made up some vows, and woke up to thousands of views and comments. It was so romantic and so us. That was wedding number one.

"Just after our online wedding, friends told us of their plans to go to the first-ever Interisland Pride Parade in Mauritius.

It was a big, big deal. Two months before Pride there, we booked our flights. And also booked our 'other' wedding. We landed on a fancy restaurant, invited a few friends (one of whom happens to be a photographer), and booked city hall for that afternoon. As is the tradition in my family, we eloped (so did my parents and two of my four siblings). It is really sweet coming into your wedding at city hall; as you are off to get married you pass a couple that just got married and congratulate them. Then, after your 30-minute wedding, the incoming couple congratulates you and the congratulations train just continues. It is really lovely. The whole experience was special because it was for us: As a same-sex couple, so much of weddings are just this heteronormative thing that doesn't have meaning for us. So we did it in a way that was truly meaningful for us. That was wedding number two.

"Then the next morning we took off to Mauritius, where our friend's mother renewed our vows on the beach. It was perfect. We had an amazing trip for three weeks (that's where our wedding budget went). It was eye-opening to be in Mauritius for Pride right after our wedding. Protesters (many of them armed) were lining the parade route. For a Canadian, it was so humbling, because it is easy to sometimes take our fundamental rights for granted. Of course we can marry who we want to. Of course I can hold my husband's hand when we're walking down the street. That was the second part of our three-continent wedding and was a really important part of our wedding. We ended our honeymoon in London, England, where our friend's mother again renewed our vows, this time in front of a British pub."

6 Guest Lists and Invitations
You're Cordially Invited ... Or Not

Like marriage, weddings are mostly fun, but do require work. This is the section of the book that will help you get your shit together and make some hard (but important) decisions. In our experience, other books and tools that we looked to when planning our weddings were extremely light on this stuff. We could find endless pages of floral inspiration, but not much on navigating the hard stuff.

PENNING YOUR GUEST LIST

And THEN my mom invited all of her second cousins and their children and our guest list literally doubled. We had to find a bigger venue and I'm still bummed about it.

My mother-in-law said that I could have my own day when my daughter got married someday, that the guest list for my wedding was really for the parents of the couple.

My parents told me that since they're paying for the bulk of the reception, they can pay for as many guests as they want.

Does any of this sound familiar? We could have literally written an entire book of comments just like these. These gems came from asking our friends what their experiences were in planning their guest list. It seems like very few couples feel pressure to have a small wedding, global pandemics notwithstanding. If anything, there can be this constant negotiation to add a few more, then a few more, to the guest list.

If you could peruse your grandparents' or great-grandparents' wedding guest lists, they would most likely be much smaller than weddings today. Small weddings of 30 to 60 guests were the norm, and they were mostly held in a place of worship, cold Jell-O-mould salad buffet included. At the turn of the 20th century, Protestant reformers encouraged Americans to shun consumerism in favour of modest, simple weddings. Few brides wore white because it is such an impractical, frivolous colour. If there was cake, it would be baked at home by someone's mother or aunt. The bride's ring would be plain, invitations would go out a week or two beforehand, and the whole shebang would be announced the following Sunday in church.

After the end of the Second World War sent more than 10 million American servicemen home, traditionalist messages encouraged women to leave their wartime jobs and double-down on futures as someone's wife. A 1961 ad for a stand mixer called the Kenwood Chef proclaims, "The Chef does everything but cook — that's what wives are for!"[78] A 1938 ad for Palmolive reminded women that "Husbands stay lovers … when wives guard against dry, lifeless skin."[79] A 1947 Pyrex ad so helpfully declared, "Successful marriages start in the kitchen."[80] The message, loud and clear, was that the nuclear family model — with breadwinning husbands and homemaking wives — was at the core of life. That dogma, coupled with an exploding advertising industry (hello, television), sent couples to the altar in record numbers. The nuclear family was revered like nothing else, and so we started to romanticize weddings.

So, just how big is the average wedding now? About 130 guests, which is 260 percent more than a wedding 60 or so years ago.[81] But really, when is it time to close the guest list? You can have a wedding for 400 people, and we can guarantee that someone will suggest that so-and-so should also be invited. You can't please them all, so please, relax. We're all for squeezing another seat around the dinner table, but how far will you extend the invitation to your wedding? 410? 490? 500 guests? Here is some truth: Your guest list will cause you grief. However, consider these, well, considerations before you put pen to paper:

- Professing a lifetime commitment to another person is pretty heavy stuff. Do you actually want strangers witnessing that?
- On your wedding day, how comfortable are you meeting someone for the first time? Seriously, play that out in your head.
- How much time do you hope to have to share with your guests that night? Check this out: If you invite 125 guests and figure, from start to finish, you have about six hours of total wedding time, you have about two minutes for every guest (hat tip to Michelle's father-in-law for the reality check on this one).
- Will you compromise on the experience, venue, and budget you want, if you let the guest list get out of hand?
- No one can purchase seats for your wedding. If you have family helping to finance your wedding, you and your fiancé should have a good sense of the size of the wedding that you want and stick to it.

WHY K AND C KEPT THEIR EYE ON THE WEDDING "SIZE" PRIZE

"Our biggest issue was deciding who to invite. We respectfully asked that plus ones be reserved for significant others or family; no strangers allowed! We stayed on budget and we expected to pay for the wedding solely from our pockets. We focused on the size of our wedding. Heterosexual weddings can have a certain pressure to be grand or bigger and better. As a same-sex couple, we didn't experience that as we went through the process of the planning, meal tasting, arranging the ceremony structure. We were content with celebrating our marriage and being grateful that we can get married in Canada. We find that it is easy to get lost sometimes in heterosexual weddings, since getting married has always been accepted as a norm. As a same-sex couple planning our wedding, we didn't take that for granted."

- Do you want a full fam-jam vibe with cute kids running around? Or do you imagine something a bit more formal and elegant, with an adults-only audience?
- Have you found a venue that is perfect, and you simply can't imagine getting married anywhere else? Its capacity might govern your guest list.

Get all this into your head and encourage your partner to do the same. Out of all the people you want to do right by in planning this guest list, you and your partner are numero uno. While compromise is key, try to balance just where that compromise is coming from.

Considering Your Guest List

Couples use all kinds of creative measurements to evaluate who should be on the guest list. Here are some questions that should help get you all the information that you need to make an informed decision:

- Do we know them as a couple, or only individually?
- Are we inviting them only because we were invited to their wedding?
- Are we genuinely stoked they'll be there, or are we taking one for the team by inviting them?
- Have we had a meal with them in the last year?
- Is there a reasonable balance of guests from each of our families and our friends?

This isn't to suggest that a formula or clear-cut criteria will solve all your problems, but it will help you find some sort of criteria to keep things contained. Mark our words, you can't please everyone. Let's say you are envisioning 75 of your nearest and dearest for your wedding, and your parents hit the roof because not all of your cousins are invited. Even if you scale up to 100 to invite them all, we guarantee that someone will be all, "Well, what about your second cousin so-and-so?" Even if you have a wedding for 300, there will be some random five guests that someone thinks you are making a mistake from not inviting. Let it go.

If you want an intimate wedding, tell your family that's what's up. When you share your guest list, remind them that you are keeping things small. The easiest way to do

The Optics of Your Guest Lists

Generally speaking, if anyone is being invited to celebrate the events leading up to your wedding, then they should be invited to the main event.

If they are close enough to you to be invited to a shower or bachelor/bachelorette, then they are close enough to come to the wedding. Consider the optics of a huge shower and bachelorette where only a third of these guests are invited to the wedding. It reeks of a gift grab, right? If you don't want to invite all of the guests to your actual wedding, consider scaling back on these parties. They aren't mandatory, after all.

that is book your venue first, so you can relay its capacity ("I know you'd love for all of my cousins to be invited, but the room only fits 50 people. We have to work within that.) Of course, say it with a smile and follow it with "I love you."

Keeping the Peace with the People You Love

Some weddings will be planned by the engaged couple. Others will be more of a family affair with a few key people (okay, typically the moms) helping to shape the big day. That means compromise, which is an excellent virtue to develop, as you'll need it in spades for the rest of your married life.

We can feel your shoulders rising up to your ears as you read this. You're thinking, "Compromise means it not being how I want it to be," and you're mostly right. But rather than having a goal of your wedding being exactly how you envision it, your goal should be building healthy relationships. Your wedding is a day. The relationships tied up in planning your wedding will last way, way longer. Don't let your wedding plant icky seeds that will one day grow into massive trees.

Negotiating with people with whom you have close, intimate relationships can be hard, but it's not impossible. "Go back to the principles of psychology, where we start with 'why,'" suggests Fotini Iconomopoulos, a negotiation and communication expert. "Start with, 'Hey, what is it that you want to get out of this day? Why is this day so important to you?' And can you explain that in an articulate way to your family and friends? 'Hey guys, we just want to make sure that our day is as intimate as possible and we have as much time to spend with everybody who's there. We don't want to get lost if we have a massive list of people.' Right? That's a great why."

If you find yourself at an impasse when you and your partner can't agree with, say, your parents or their parents, you must approach it as a united front. You know when you board an airplane and in the safety check they caution to put your own oxygen mask on first, before helping others? You and your beloved get the oxygen mask first. Once you

A COUPLE REINS IN AN ENTHUSIASTIC FATHER-IN-LAW

"I just got engaged. We decided on a super-small wedding. As soon as we told our family about our engagement, my father-in-law got on the phone and started telling his entire extended family to start looking into flights! When we gently reminded him that we want a small wedding, he brushed us off and offered to pay for as many guests as he would like to invite. It wasn't the cost that prompted us to want a small wedding, it was the intimacy. So, we stepped up our venue search and put a deposit down on a restaurant that has a capacity of 50 people. Then, we Facetimed them to say that we totally fell in love with a venue and locked in a date. We said it can only fit 50 people including us, so we're back with the original plan of a small wedding. He got it. He wasn't thrilled, but he got it. Then at our wedding he was the first and last person on the dance floor and had the best time. It wasn't an issue and never came up again."

and your betrothed are on the same page, greet your families with big hearts. They have all the best intentions. If things are getting heated or you suspect someone doesn't have such good intentions after all, face it as a couple, with the person closest to the issue leading the discussion.

If your parents start to act a fool, it should be you, not your partner, who is having a talk with them. Likewise, if your soon-to-be-in-laws are being offside, your partner should lead the discussion with them.

You should plan to make your decisions known well in advance — that is, if you've planned a long engagement. If you're going from engagement to wedding quite quickly, still try to give loved ones a bit

A BRIDE FINDS MIDDLE GROUND WITH IN-LAWS

Crystal felt the heat of trying to please her soon-to-be in-laws. "When we told them we wanted a small wedding, they offered to host a party for us, then once they started looking at costs, they ditched that idea! We both felt some serious pressure, in particular from my MIL, on our guest list. She treated our wedding like a do-over for her own. She started getting really pushy during the wedding process, weirdly about a registry. We didn't want one, we had lived together for years and had all the stuff we wanted. She maintained that it would make it easier for people to shop. I asked her, 'Who is the shower really for? Us or for other people?!' It was awkward. We ended up registering for a honeymoon and travel stuff — basically to pacify people. Now that I'm a mother, I wish I was softer with my MIL."

of time to get used to your perhaps "non-traditional" approach, but that might not always be the case. So, give yourself at least a week or two to make such monumental announcements, then, if required, take a day or two to reset if something goes sideways with a loved one. Give them enough time to become more level-headed, and then reach out one more time before the wedding. Hopefully, things won't be as tense and you won't have to make any drastic cuts to the wedding, and also your life.

Because that's the crux, isn't it? If you cut someone from your wedding guest list, they likely are cut from your life, as well. We're not saying it's not possible, but that is one big hurdle for two friends or loved ones to get over. So be cautious and be kind.

Inviting Adults Only

You might hit some friction if you want an adults-only wedding. Children are adorable and awesome, and you'll surely be reminded of that the day after the wedding when the pressure for grandkids sets in! Seriously though, not every wedding is kid-friendly and that's okay. If you have your heart set on a romantic candlelit ceremony at 10 p.m., then there's a tacit understanding that it is a grown-up, adults-only wedding. Everyone will get it, right? Well, maybe.

If you get a reply back that RSVPs for children that weren't invited, get on the phone. Don't text, email, or write a letter. Whoever is closest to them needs to pick up the phone and have an awkward conversation that goes something like this: "We got your RSVP and are really happy you can come! This is awkward, but we had hoped that you and John could come, we didn't plan on the kids coming. It is a late-night wedding/very small wedding/adults-only wedding/insert reason here and we can't accommodate kids. We totally understand if this means you can't come. We hope you can, but we get it."

One of us, who shall not be named, actually asked for no kids at their wedding, and had a relative bring their little one without asking. Not a huge deal in the long run, but it made other guests question the no kid's rule — like, "why weren't my kids invited?" The only person who looks like a jerk in this scenario is neither of the two people getting married, we might add.

If a random baby does show up at your nuptials, it's best to be gracious and ignore this little faux pas. Because, as moms now ourselves, we do understand not wanting to leave a little one, especially when they are really little, behind. In fact, the mom may have not even noticed the no kids rule on the invitation — #mombrain #momfog #newmomlife. Breastfeeding or not, when they're that little it's sometimes hard to find a babysitter or someone you trust to watch them.

On the flip side, if a friend or family member has RSVPed yes to your big day and they, like, JUST had a baby, reach out pre-wedding to see if they need help facilitating a babysitter or if they have any

COMMUNICATION IS KEY FOR ADULT-ONLY INVITES

If you have your heart set on a venue not really conducive to little ones toddling about, stick to your guns. Mollify any potential hurt feelings by sharing your intentions in a clear but gentle manner.

1. Plant the seed early. As early as possible into your planning, lay the foundation by sharing that the affair will be adults-only.
2. Be firm. As the question will inevitably come up, treat it as an opportunity to let people know and do it with conviction.
3. Choose your words carefully. The difference between "we have decided" and "we are thinking about" leaves too much room for interpretation. Be very clear in your diction.
4. Ensure your invitations reflect your plans. Address invitations to precisely whom they are intended for, meaning specific individuals or couples, rather than families.
5. Tell everyone. You and your partner should both tell your close friends, family, and wedding party your plans, so the word will spread quickly, and not only through you.
6. Avoid disparaging children. Focus on the elements of the wedding that are decidedly grown-up (perhaps an elegant menu, or your favourite champagne).
7. No flower girl or ringbearer. Be mindful that your guests who have left their own children at home might be surprised — and, let's be honest, miffed — to see children in your wedding party — and rightly so. It is all or nothing when it comes to an adults-only wedding.

questions about the facilities. This will act as a gentle reminder to the bleary new parents that you have instilled a no-child policy around the date and will also help them feel taken care of at a time when up is down, and baby poop is their main topic of conversation. The new mom may need a quiet room to pump breastmilk and/or call the sitter for a baby debrief/check-in. On top of that, if momma is giving life through her newly voluptuous chest, she may also have some dietary restrictions to contend with that may not have been an issue when the couple said yes to attending your wedding.

Inviting Plus Ones

Partners or spouses of friends or family members are a cinch when it comes to sending out invites, but what about your single guests? There is often pressure to address invitations to a single recipient with "and guest," but are you obliged to? While it is a thoughtful gesture to allow a single guest to bring a date, it is not required. Particularly if you have your heart set on a small-ish wedding, or venue capacity is an issue, you don't need to extend a plus one. That said, it is nice. If you've been to a wedding as a single guest, it can sting. Come on, nothing rubs a little salt into one's single status like an entire evening celebrating romance and coupledom. Before making a final decision though, here are three careful considerations to keep in mind:

- The same rule should apply to all guests, so either all single guests are welcome to bring a date, or no one is. It is only fair.
- Just how many single guests will there be at your wedding? If it is a matter of adding two or three guests, it might be a feasible and a very kind gesture. Your single friends will likely have a better time if they can bring along a guest.
- Are you comfortable meeting someone for the first time at your wedding? Such an intimate occasion might not be the ideal setting to be making introductions.

One recent bride, Sheila, was totally comfortable giving plus ones a hard no. "I basically didn't want to meet anyone for the first time at my own wedding. I've been a guest and being introduced to the couple at their own wedding is so awkward. When we got married we had about 10 single friends and we were like 'Nope, sorry, no plus ones.' People got it. They understood," she said.

If you are put on the spot and a guest asks about bringing along a date, you can politely decline by explaining you have limited seating or aren't comfortable meeting new people on such a monumental day. And if there are many guests coming solo to your wedding, perhaps use the opportunity to suggest they save a dance for a certain other guest? Romance will be in the air, after all.

Acknowledging the Grief that Is Modern Families

Most modern families have some degree of complexity: a divorce, estranged family member, people no longer on speaking terms … you get the idea. The Perfect Wedding doesn't seem to have a lot of room for imperfect families. Weddings don't smooth out family drama, they often draw it to the surface. Decades-old issues of divorced parents might suddenly feel raw. A relationship with an estranged family member might suddenly be in the spotlight as you have to decide whether or not to invite them.

If you have to contend with this, listen, we feel for you. It sucks that your wedding will (likely) force some awkward conversations. We can't tell you who to invite or whose invitations should get lost in the mail, but we can tell you to find some otherworldly patience and deal with it head on. If there is a deep wedge in your family and you're not sure whether or not to invite someone, consider this: purposefully leaving someone out of your wedding will calcify the relationship; inviting them might soften years, even decades, of estrangement.

If your parents' divorce tore your family in half and they refuse to speak, have separate conversations with them. Tell them how much it stresses you out and how you just want everyone (for one goddamn day) to put the past in the past and focus on the future of your family, which involves your wedding. Cry, confide, explain — do whatever lifts this weight from your shoulders, but do it in a gentle, empathetic way. If it is hard for you to say, imagine how hard it is for a parent to hear.

Despite all that emotional labour, things still might not go your way. Getting married might build some bridges in your relationships and it might not. Some people cannot and will not get along just because you are getting married and, as hard as it is to concede, you can't be responsible for how other people feel or act.

Getting married will also put a magnifying glass on your own relationship. If there was tension about money before you decided to get married, it will surely be more tense. If you are stressed about controlling in-laws before you get engaged, that will likely increase. Despite every rom-com, Hollywood wedding, or Disney fantasy, happily ever after comes with some strings. There's almost certainly going to be a disconnect between how you expect getting married and married life will be, and how it actually is. Weddings are supposed to be happy, romantic, and special, when in reality, they can be stressful, expensive, and mind-numbingly tedious to plan — if you let them.

CREATING YOUR INVITATIONS

How you invite people to your wedding does set the tone for what guests are in for, but invitations can be overrated. We've never stepped foot in a craft store, which immediately ruled us out for DIY invitations, but that doesn't mean we don't appreciate gorgeous stationery. Wedding invitations can be beautiful. They can also be fussy and outrageously overpriced. Before you order a set of invitations that will run you $40 (CDN) per guest, including an embossed map of where to park and a hand-calligraphed RSVP card, check this out: The purpose of your invitation is to ask people to come to your wedding, confirm their attendance, and provide them with details.

A BRIDE'S MOM LOST IT OVER THE BEER ON HER MENU

"I come from a working-class family in a small town in Northern Ontario. I ended up in New York. Not only did I end up falling in love with the city, but *in* the city. We couldn't imagine getting married anywhere else. By the time we were planning a wedding, we had been living in Brooklyn for almost 10 years. My mom had been to visit me once. She wasn't shy about telling me how much she hated where I lived. She came down the month before the wedding to spend some time with us and it was tense. The tension kept building, but I didn't dare bring it up because I just wanted us to have a nice visit.

One afternoon, my boyfriend and I brought her over to the venue where we were getting married. I thought it would be fun to show her the space and taste some of the food together. I think I was trying to create some sort of special memory for both of us so I could be like, 'See? Remember, we did that thing together!' As soon as we got to the venue, she started talking about how expensive things were, and why did we need all this fancy stuff. What finally blew her stack was that she couldn't get a Bud Light. It was bad enough that we were getting married down here and wanted nice wines and a signature cocktail or two, but it was too much that she couldn't have a domestic beer. She put it on pretty thick, saying that my uncles and brothers wouldn't have fun because they are beer-drinking men. I was embarrassed. It struck a nerve that wasn't anything to do with beer. This was about the fact that she felt out of place and I wasn't on her side anymore. The rest of her visit had this cloud over it, and we didn't talk about it until I went home for Christmas about four months after the wedding. She had this vision of what my wedding was going to be like and when I didn't hit the mark, we had to work that all out."

Before you go down the rabbit hole on how to word an invitation while taking into account two sets of divorced parents, just get the details down. Like, the nitty gritty details. What time are you getting married? Where is the ceremony? Where is the reception, and at what time? Is there dinner and dancing (code for guests will be fed) or cocktails and canapés (cues your guests to have a snack before they come). How do people confirm their attendance? Is the wording clear that the entire family is invited, or just the adults, and the children should be left with a babysitter that night?

These are the details that *actually* matter. What doesn't matter, contrary to popular opinion, is what colour the invites are, foiled or embossed font, or if they match your table settings.

If you are a graphic designer or an artist, maybe the invitations and stationery are really important to you. Alison Slight, a luxury event planner in Toronto, notes that a lot of people invest in this area, but not a ton of guests will notice, so only you can decide if it is worth it.

Looking Past the Post

Yes, you can invite people to your wedding through means other than mail. The wedding police will not come for you. Yes, you can call guests with the details. Gasp! You might be thinking: Where's the formality or sense of occasion in that? Back in the day, when there was a really important event, people were invited in person, either by the host, or by a page. So if you're feeling pressured into paying for 100-pound test embossed paper just because it is the "right" thing to do, you can liberate yourself from that. You can invite people to your wedding however you want.

Times are changing and invitations are long overdue for modernization. They aren't cheap, aren't great for the environment, and seem superfluous. Seriously, everyone makes all of their plans using their phone. It is just how we socialize now. Phone calls are considered intimate now, right? When someone actually calls us and we think "Ugh, why not just text me?" Hell, by comparison an evite feels special! If you're reading this and thinking, "Yeah, our wedding is too formal

Sending Save-the-Date Cards

Want to know the most foolproof way to get people to save the date for your wedding? Invite them to your wedding.

Save-the-date cards are effective for two things: killing trees and wasting money. People look at them and maybe, *maybe* toss the date in their calendar. Just invite them for heaven's sake. Look, if someone already has plans on the day you're getting married, they're either going to cancel them or they're not.

Just pull your shit together and invite people about eight weeks before your wedding.

for an evite, we're going full-on-black-tie," we feel you. Your invitation should match your wedding, no question. Get as fancy as you want.

If you're into a printed invitation but not into investing a ton, there are lots of budget-friendly options online that you can design and print in a snap. Invitations can be an area where you find some savings in your budget. When it comes to timing, plan to get your invitations out about two months before your wedding.

If you are ordering custom stationery like RSVP and thank-you cards, build in a few weeks to shop around and find something you like. We'll help you with the wording in a bit, but in the meantime pay attention to size and weight. If you fall in love with a card that isn't standard postage size, or if it is carved from wood, it is going to cost a fortune to mail. You can knock yourself out with paper stock, fonts, gatefolds, and flourishes galore — just find something that you like and that fits your budget. If you geek out over engraving, you might want to build this into your invite budget. If not, laser printing can still look gorgeous.

Build in ample time to get these addressed, stamped, and in the mail. When you're looking at how many to order, plan to send one invitation to the person or household invited and order a few extras (both invites and envelopes) just in case. Pop a few extras away for your 50th wedding anniversary. Awwwwwww.

If you are inviting people through other means (we're here for it), do it two months before the wedding and you're in good shape. Whichever way you invite people, even digitally, we beseech you to have someone else proofread your invitation. Many invitations have been printed with typos that people didn't catch on the first or even second read-through.

Working Around Remarriages, Deaths, and Divorces

There is a perception that a wedding invitation should come from the bride's parents. It's not a rule. Let's be real: Most weddings happen as a result of lots of people chipping in financially and otherwise. If a family member is financially contributing to your wedding, they don't have naming rights.

More couples getting married today are dealing with some sort of family dynamic that's causing them some stress. Parents who have divorced, remarried, or someone who has passed away. Or you're two brides or two grooms getting hitched, or for whatever reason this traditional gendered shit isn't working for you.

Don't stress this and go do something fun instead (like have sex with your partner!). Use this all-encompassing and beautifully inclusive line: *Together with their families.* There. No hierarchy. No order of names to worry about. No attempt to try to pay tribute to a parent who has passed. Just an honest, easy line. You two, getting hitched, with your families, are inviting your guests.

Hot Tip: Recycle Those Gift Registry Cards

Recycle those cards immediately. They are tacky. Including your registry information in your invitation has a whiff of entitlement about it. Your wedding is not everyone's first rodeo. Most people know that when they come to a wedding, they bring a gift to the couple. They get it. If people want to know where you registered, they'll ask for it. So instead of putting the "please buy us a gift from here" cards in your invitations, just tell your closest friends and your family where you registered.

Addressing Those Invitations

If you ever host a ball or white-tie gala, this will come in handy.

The most formal way to invite someone is also the least feminist. We kept our last names after we got married, so we don't love it when someone addresses us at Mrs. Husband's so-and-so. We're big, big fans of our husbands, but we're our own people with our own names. If you want to address your invitations formally, might we suggest using Ms. and the woman's full name? Ms. is like Mr. There is no married or single connotation. There is no equivalent of Miss (single) or Mrs. (married) for dudes, so we think that's fair.

Here are a few examples of how that looks:

- Mr. Simon and Ms. Emmeline Bee (if they share a surname; or, to be more conservative, Mr. Simon and Mrs. Emmeline Bee)
- Ms. Emmeline Bunny and Mr. Simon Bee (if they don't share a surname)
- Dr. Emmeline Bunny and Mr. Simon Bee (if one is a doctor)
- Doctors Emmeline Bunny and Simon Bee (if both happen to be doctors)
- The Honourable Simon Bee and Lieutenant Emmeline Bunny, Royal Canadian Air Force (if they have distinguished titles as a judge, an ambassador, serviceperson, or elected official)

For same-sex couples, address alphabetically by surname: Mr. Simon Bee and Mr. Charles Bunny.

For same-sex women, the default is often Ms., though many couples are happily embracing Mrs.

For people or couples that identify as nonbinary, go with Mx.

When in doubt, you can just ask!

If you want to call out little people on the invitation (nice touch), some traditionalists recommend addressing girls under 18 as "Miss" and that boys are addressed as "Master" until they are 18 — at which point they're addressed as "Mr." We don't like the gender imbalance there, so if you're going with Miss for a girl, use Mr. for her brother. Or, let's all relax and call kids by their first names.

Real-Life Wedding Stories

C and M chose austerity measures in order to have what they wanted.

"Our wedding plans changed and evolved as we figured out the sort of wedding that we wanted. We ended up having two parties that day. The first was a small daytime ceremony and reception in a private room at a really gorgeous restaurant for about 60 people. It was cocktails and canapés and pretty fabulous. It was under $10K (CDN) and I would have been happy if that was it. But it was too small and our guest list outpaced the venue.

"So, we had a second party that night that was about 140 people at a brewery. That party was almost $20K (CDN). While we were getting costs, we were very clear that it was either a wedding or our financial future.

"We were looking at a venue where we could bring in a liquor licence and do it all from scratch, but it was actually cheaper and totally turnkey to do it at a restaurant. We debated city hall and a ton of other options. I knew it meant a lot to my family, particularly my mom's side (my aunts), so we had a party. Before we knew what anything costs, we were ready to spend $20K (CDN). Then we realized what that got us, and we scaled up our budget and our savings. We saved $500 (CDN) each from each paycheque, so about $2,000 (CDN) each month.

"We were totally floored by the expense of it all, but found, surprisingly, that invitations were pretty reasonable. I did mine on Minted Weddings and they weren't at all expensive. All the paper and bullshit and stamps. It's silly. We didn't do mail-in reply cards, we set up an email address.

"I didn't want to have the same wedding that everyone else has. I wanted different music, decor, different everything. We were totally on the same page when it came to the budget and wedding planning. He really wanted a wedding website and a limo, I didn't care. The two of us planned it in lockstep.

"I still listen to the playlist we made together for the wedding and I always cry when I hear it. It really felt like us.

"If I could give any couple advice, it is that it is not about the wedding. It's one thing. Yeah, it's nice, they are great for families, but it's not about the wedding. It is about the marriage."

D and K kept things quick and on the smaller side, focusing on the fun parts of getting married.

"We got married a bit later in life and had been to countless weddings together. They were all special in their own way, but there was a lot of stuff that didn't feel relevant to us. We sat down and made a list of all of the usual trappings, decided which felt like us and took a big red Sharpie to all the things that didn't. That meant a yes to an evening candlelit reception at a winery for about 50 people. We booked the winery then told our family about it.

"It went like this: 'Good news! We have a date and a place where we're getting married! But the place is super tiny, so we'll let you know where we're at with the guest list soon!' We called people to invite them, no invitations.

"We went pretty formal. He wore a tux and I wore a floor-length slip dress but not a veil or bouquet. We got ready together (because we always get ready together) over a glass of wine. He made sure the back of my hair looked good, I helped him get his bowtie just right.

"We got married at 8 p.m., and about 15 minutes before that we asked my brother and my husband's best friend to be our witnesses — no walking down the aisle, no wedding party. We wanted a super agnostic ceremony that was romantic and short, and it was.

"After we were officially married, the music was turned up and it was a great little party. No first dance. No cake cutting. No formal pictures. No speeches, although there were some really lovely impromptu tipsy toasts toward the end of the night. We had our favourite food truck roll up around midnight. Then, when it was time to call it a night, we ordered a ton of cars to get people home safely. It was absolutely the most perfect night. We didn't spend a dollar more than we wanted to. We didn't do or participate in anything that didn't feel like us."

7 Overspending
Our Relationship with Money Gets Complicated

The modern wedding is often the single largest expense many families will ever have, up there with going to school or a down payment on a car or home. And yet of those three milestone expenses, only two are typically sage, long-term investments.

If this strikes you as backward or misguided, good. Your wedding doesn't have to be like that. These are five inarguable truths, nay, mantras, that you can repeat throughout your entire wedding planning process:

- We can have an awesome wedding and not drain our savings in the process.
- Our wedding is not worth going into debt over.
- We will need to choose some priorities in order to create and stick to a budget.
- Our wedding is not a reason to go on a spending spree.
- Our marriage will get off on a better foot if we are on the same page about wedding costs.

Now repeat those 10 times while staring deeply into your partner's eyes and commit them to memory. Just kidding. Sort of. We hope that by just getting acquainted with these principles, you'll feel empowered to make decisions that are financially sound while planning this day.

FEELING THE PRESSURE FOR EXTRAVAGANCE

There's no question that weddings today are more extravagant than they were only three or four decades ago, but why? There's a little one-upwomanship happening. Gender and sexuality professor Dr. Andrea O'Reilly posits that hyper-consumerist display is tied to a sort of display or performance of showing you have money. "There is pressure to show that you have made it," she says of weddings. It certainly feels like nowadays there is more focus on the prettiness of the wedding and flaunting its photo-worthiness than on the significance of the union.

Josh Spiegel, creative director at NY-based Birch Event Design, says that in the good old days (okay, like, 10 years ago), the idea was to find an amazing venue and use all the venue's stuff. "You'd add your centrepieces to their table but that was it. It was fine, everyone was happy. Now, it is about an experience. It went from just bringing in centrepieces to bringing in linens, all your tableware, and glasses, to custom dance floors, staging a new bar, hiring new bartenders. Every detail is taken into account, like walking into a hotel where everyone is helpful and good looking. Everything is custom."[82] To what end do couples try to keep up?

The princess-ification (yes, we likely just made up that term) of brides is also literal wedding inspiration. Disney, arguably the de facto creator of the princess as we know it, is in the wedding business. And not in a small way. They might not be able to find you a Prince Charming, but they sure can get you hitched like Cinderella — for a royal fee. You can get married at Disney's Wedding Pavilion, nestled on its own island in a lagoon (accessible by, what else, a footbridge) with sweeping views of your — sorry, we mean Cinderella's — castle. To have a wedding ceremony in front of Cinderella's castle at Disney World, which can accommodate 100 guests at a ceremony time of 9:30 a.m., there is a $30,000 (USD) minimum cost.[83] The reception is *entirely* separate. Well, everything is separate.

Want Mickey and Minnie to make a cameo? $1,700 (USD). Want a white-dove flyover? $250 (USD). A private firework display and dessert party? $2,500 (USD). Roll up to the wedding in Cinderella's horse-drawn crystal coach, driven by a Major Domo? $4,700 (USD). An English butler to deliver your wedding bands in Cinderella's glass slipper? $800 (USD). Want to celebrate with 300 of your nearest and dearest after-hours in front of the Cinderella castle? $180,000 (USD), minimum.[84] Of course, if you want to pop the question or renew your proposal (is renewing proposals a thing? Apparently at Disney it is), magical moments can also be arranged for a fee.

SUSSING OUT THOSE SNEAKY WEDDING MARKUPS

Want to play a fun game? It is called Guess the Profit Margin! When you buy a cake, it's $30 (CDN). When you buy a wedding cake, it is $300 (CDN)! Oooh, gorgeous silk gown in black? $300 (CDN). That same dress in white, add a zero or two.

If you take the attire and the ceremony out of the equation, the budgeting formula of your event is like any other huge party. Any big celebration (a huge milestone birthday, for example) needs the same "stuff": music, food, drinks, decor, and maybe someone to take some photos. So why does the same thing cost more just because it is a wedding? As the wedding industry continues to snowball out of control, couples are being taken advantage of, big time.

And according to a report by online registry website Zola, a whopping 96 percent of the 500 recently engaged or newlywed couples they surveyed across the U.S. said that wedding planning is stressful. Almost half of those used the words *very* or *extremely* to describe it.[85]

The biggest stressor? Naturally, it was creating and sticking to the budget. Money matters can put strain on a relationship at the best of times. Add in the additional anxiety of getting hitched and you've got a volcano essentially waiting to erupt thanks to your bank accounts.

What's romantic about money stress? Absolutely nothing.

UNDERSTANDING HOW MONEY, MARRIAGE, AND EMOTION MEET

Megan Ford is a clinic director, financial therapist, and financial therapy researcher at the University of Georgia's ASPIRE Clinic. She is the author of Finding Harmony, a blog that explores any array of couples and money topics. Ford is also part of a growing group of professionals focusing their work and research on the crossovers between marriage, families, and finances — aka financial therapy. The intersection of relationships and money is, obviously, a hot and very necessary topic when facing down a wedding budget, and one's financial future, as a couple.

The stress of having a "perfect" wedding is anchored in a few areas, says Ford.[86] "Primarily for women, there is this pervasive narrative, this long-standing belief of what a wedding means. From a very young age, we receive this message over and over again that it is the happiest day of our life. The 'big day.' Particularly for girls, there is this idea that a wedding is a major, major event and you need to have it together. That is a lot of buildup and pressure to put on one day. Another factor is the stress rooted in familial pressure and cultural influences that dictate how a wedding should be — we draw a lot of meaning from our families and cultures of origin." When these things conflict, it is a recipe for tension. "Parents might have different ideas of what a wedding should be than their children. Or both sets of parents might have very different views. There are different story lines that make for the perfect day, and the definition of perfection is different," explains Ford.

"As people set out to plan their wedding, recognize those narratives around them. If we are unaware of what is influencing us, we can't find the level of reason required to navigate this space. We need to find grounding. That's an important thing for couples to reflect on," Ford advises.

Ford also points out that how a wedding fits into a financial plan is largely dictated by who is paying for the wedding. Even if that isn't the couple getting married, the cost of the wedding is surely affecting someone's financial plan. Someone is footing the bill. "This can be a generational issue, for example, imagine a mother that really wants her daughter to be able to have a lavish wedding, but it means sacrificing their own financial stability. That's pretty heavy stuff. You might find that people and families that are otherwise very financially reasonable get caught up in the frenzy. It can lead to decisions that feel right in the moment, but don't necessarily reflect the future ramifications because we are solely focused on the big day. It is easy to get sucked in and lose one's sense of grounding, especially when there are lots of voices from cultural narratives, your family, your in-laws, and the wedding industry."

TALKING FRANKLY ABOUT LONG-TERM FINANCIAL GOALS

Ford's advice is to look at things from a macro perspective and think long-term. "It is hard to zoom out when you're challenged so much by the potential excitement you might be feeling. It is really important

TREAT YOUR WEDDING LIKE ANY OTHER EVENT

Sheila and her husband approached their wedding budget like a work budget. They looked for areas to trim, but they also kept it tight and didn't go over budget. "Working in PR, I sent all my initial emails to vendors from my work email address, so I'd be getting rates comparable to if I were planning a work event, with no inherent wedding markup."

They pulled in friends to help: A friend DJed with their laptop, another friend did the flowers the day before the wedding with flowers she bought at a local store. They found some great efficiencies with photography, too. "We wanted a photojournalism-type look, capturing great moments with our friends laughing. I didn't want our wedding photos to look like everyone else's. I emailed a photographer that shot photos for a magazine that I read. He hooked us up with a great husband-and-wife team who took exactly the sort of photos we were after. We booked them but really stripped things back. Instead of paying for their hourly rate for hours and hours, we had friends snap some photos of us getting ready. We didn't need them to be the last people at the reception, either, so saved some money by not keeping them there all night."

They also budgeted for the wedding with the assumption that they'd be paying for it. "I was very uncomfortable with my parents paying for the wedding. They said, 'Look, we'll give you X dollars toward the wedding, you'll have to pay for the rest of it.' I had a really hard time accepting their money. With money comes expectations of decision-making power. I also didn't want them to feel like, here you go, this is what we gave your sister, your

> wedding can be just like hers. Fortunately, they were very easygoing, very supportive, and very focused on what we wanted to do as a couple, as opposed to couples you hear of who can't invite their friends because their parents and parents-in-law want to invite so many of their own friends. I don't come from a family where my wedding felt like it was for my parents."

to start habits before you are faced with wedding planning. I advise couples to talk early and talk often. It's going to be difficult for couples to start anew while in the excitement that is wedding planning. It is important to try and build that foundation prior to the wedding."

Don't let the cost of the wedding follow you in the future when you have other important financial goals like travelling, moving, career decisions, buying a home, starting a family. Yes, we want to have this special day AND reach our financial goals.

"Couples need to have more frank conversations from the very beginning. If one is not used to managing money, or having a budget, then having a wedding budget is going to be very hard. But this is bigger than a wedding: Creating and sticking to a budget is a key for living a successful adult life. Those skills need to be prioritized."

Ford illustrates that some really interesting dynamics can play out based on how couples approach money. One such thing is how a wedding can prompt behavioural change, this idea that someone who in everyday life is very financially practical decides that since they're only going to get married once they should buy a $10,000 dress. "The frenzy of weddings has that power, to make some people change their behaviour for one occasion. Practically, if couples feel like they need help getting themselves on the rails, they should check out some of the great online budgeting tools designed for wedding planning (but watch out for those credit card promotions). NerdWallet is a good (free!) one because it has a ton of good information and walks you through average expenses based on wedding stats to give you a sense of where your budget falls."

It is easy to get caught up in the excitement and the frenzy. The bill at the end feels like the farthest thing away from what you're feeling while planning the wedding, but make no mistake, that bill is coming. The financial stress of the wedding doesn't need to follow you into the future and, in fact, if it does, it might actually perpetuate conflict. We get very dreamy about weddings and it isn't that you can't enjoy the moment. Be dreamy, but some practicality and some realization of the future ramifications of your decisions are important.

Ford also cautions that before you are putting wedding charges on your credit card, have an honest conversation about whether you can pay it off. "With interest, that $2,000 wedding dress is now costing you $2,400. People don't think about it in the moment. Think through more practically, what can we afford without burying ourselves in debt?"

The reality is that most couples fight about money and plenty of couples divorce over it. A review of 115 studies about divorce found that couples that argue about finances at least once a week are 30 percent more likely to get divorced.[87]

Finance writer Melissa Leong says that disagreements about money are inevitable, but that doesn't necessarily make them problematic. It can be normal, healthy, and actually good to hash this all out. "You are two different people with completely different upbringings, values, and thoughts about money. Part of getting together is discussing this. Disagreements about money can still be healthy," she says. Because even if the disagreement is about money, it is always about more than just money. We all grow up with ideas about money, thoughts, values, and baggage that we, of course, bring to our marriages. Her advice is to always seek understanding. "Ask 'Why?'" Your partner is adamant about spending top dollar to treat 400 guests at the wedding. Why? What did she learn about money when she was growing up? What will it mean to her? Is it about generosity or pride or appearances or community?"[88]

REALIZING THAT WEDDINGS ARE REALLY JUST PARTIES

Weddings are like any other event, really. The only thing that's different is that you're going to stand up and say, "I do" and sign some documents. Everything else is the same: You're going to need a venue, catering, and decorations.

Alison Slight, an event designer and planner, says she encourages couples to move away from traditional pressure and make decisions that work for them. "We always start with an intake discussion. We ask: What are your priorities? What do you like? If someone is really into food, we can do it in a really beautiful restaurant and keep the numbers low. Or if scale is really important to them, we can find a space like a ballroom or brick and beam warehouse."

"For us," continues Slight, "that means an exemplification of your personality through the event execution. If people arrive and they can tell it is YOU, then you really hit the nail on the head. You need to make choices that feel appropriate for your lifestyle and your taste." She points to one scenario as an example, "If you're a super casual person, always in jeans and sneakers, then for your guests to walk into a wedding that has an explosion of flowers at a really ostentatious venue, that isn't going to feel real. There are ways to connect that authenticity from your daily vibe to your wedding." Rather than look outside for inspiration, look to yourselves.

Slight also recommends looking well outside of the wedding industry for inspiration. "Wedding magazines are so heavily driven by advertisers in the industry, readers might look at those as a guide for what's trendy, not knowing that there are advertisers behind the content."

The perennial truth of any party is that people always remember if there was enough to eat and drink. "People with a drink in their hand are happy people. People looking for a drink will always complain. Put the bar near the entrance," Slight recommends.

SAVING BEFORE YOU START SPENDING

As soon as you decide to get married, go beast mode when it comes to savings, advises Leong, author of the award-winning finance guide *Happy Go Money*. Cut back on expenditures, big time. "Tell your friends that you're saving for your wedding so everyone is on board — and they can cheer you on instead of peer pressuring you to come out for dinner every weekend. Pick up some extra shifts at work or consider taking up a side hustle for extra money. It doesn't have to be forever. It's just for your goals," she says. There is no "right" length of time to save for your wedding, you have to do what works for you and your budget. But be aware that the longer you have to save, the easier it might be for your budget to creep! Stick to that budget.

And no pussyfooting about money. Get matter-of-fact about it really quick. "When it comes to money, I'm all about being forthright. More people should talk about money so that it's out in the open and there are no misunderstandings. First, I would start with a conversation with your spouse-to-be so that you're on the same page about your expectations and your wedding budget. Then bring your plans to your family members. They may be more receptive to any requests if they see that you've put some meaningful thought — and real calculations — into the celebration," Leong cautions.

A wedding budget doesn't exist in a vacuum: it is one part of your overall financial plan. Leong explains that there's no time like the present to start long-term planning. "A wedding can sometimes be the first time a couple even talks about dollars and cents. It can be a great opportunity to discuss your future goals together." When you and your beloved look to your post-wedding future, what do you want? Do you want to buy a condo? Have children? Go out to dinner several times a week? Go away on a trip every year? Talking about your big-picture goals will help you zoom out and see how your wedding fits into your financial plans. "When we were planning the wedding, my husband and I had an important conversation about debt," says Leong. "How did we feel about debt? Were we okay with starting our lives together with debt from our wedding? Ultimately, we were not."

Keeping a tight budget isn't just important for your financial future, duh, it might also save your marriage. The ability to save together and financially plan for your wedding is good discipline that might help keep you together: a study found that couples who save together are more likely to stay together.[89] Cheers to that!

Blowing Your Budget Might Mess with Your Marriage

Couples who spend big bucks on their weddings are more likely to get divorced than those who stick to tighter budgets.[*] A 2014 study found that weddings costing less than $1,300 (CDN) showed a significant decrease in the likelihood of divorce compared with those that cost over $26,000 (CDN) (which is particularly interesting, as the average wedding was more than $30,000 [CDN].)[†]

CHECKING YOUR GUT ON WHY WE WANT WHAT WE (THINK) WE WANT

Joan DiFuria, co-founder and director of the Money, Meaning & Choices Institute in California, encourages couples to carefully take stock. "If you have the money and can afford a lavish wedding, and it is something that is meaningful and important to you, go for it. But before you jump in, get real with yourself on why this is important to you. Is this coming from an inner place, one that's rooted in financial literacy and self-respect? Or is this about keeping up with the Joneses and trying to project a certain image?"[90]

She touches on something very seductive, which is the temptation to blow the bank when times are good and happy. Leong says it's like

---

[*] Andrew Francis-Tan and Hugo M. Mialon, "'A Diamond Is Forever,' and Other Fairy Tales: The Relationship Between Wedding Expenses and Marriage Duration," *Economic Inquiry* 53, no. 4 (September 2014) 1919–30.

[†] Thiago Loureiro, "How Much Does the Average Canadian Wedding Actually Cost?" Slice, August 25, 2014, slice.ca/weddings/blog/how-much-does-the-average-canadian-wedding-actually-cost/63019.

having the wedding blinders on. "It's your WEDDING so your eyes glaze over the price tags because this is your dream, your family's big show, cultural tradition, and it only happens once in your life so go all out. The industry understands that the sky's the limit when it comes to money and responds accordingly."

"Here's the thing," notes DiFuria. "Starting a marriage is a positive and monumental milestone in life. In those powerfully positive moments in life, it is easy to say, Spend! Go big! Do it however you want! But let's be honest: Half of marriages don't last. So, what do you want from this: the experience of having a wedding or a secure financial future that sets your marriage off on a good foot? Because you pay for that experience of a wedding and you can't get a refund. Emotionally or financially."

Recently married, Alice knew a wedding would be expensive, but she didn't imagine just how quickly costs would escalate.[91] "Sometimes I think, I wish we had the money. People think that financially you might break even at your wedding or even come out ahead. We didn't come close to it. It is not because people weren't generous, they were, very much so. It just was what it was. You pay through the nose for every single thing. You're being taken advantage of and being upsold at every opportunity. We flew in flowers from Holland, for fuck's sake. WHY?"

Why do we think it's okay to drain our bank accounts in order to have a good time? And moreover, where does this arms race of wedding one-upmanship come from? DiFuria calls it like she sees it. "We can't blame companies for being companies. We exist in a capitalist society. There is a market and it takes two. We continue to normalize and panegyrize the over-the-topness of weddings (and all the things that go along with them), and we buy more and more and more of it." And, of course, in response the market continues to rise to that demand.

DiFuria points out that if you come to the table with a strong sense of self, you should be able to get through your wedding without feeling like someone else. "One's values about the saving and spending of money prior to the wedding should not change dramatically once the wedding party is planned," she believes. If there is a dramatic change in values, that is a red flag. "Do you have the internal boundaries, and a strong enough sense of self, to help determine how much is spent on those four or five hours of life? If someone has a strong sense of identity and a psychologically strong sense of self, and is solid about the saving and spending of money, they will more likely move toward a wedding party that is meaningful from the inside out not the outside in," she says.

"Couples need to get real with themselves — as a couple and as individuals," she continues. "You will wake up after your wedding and think about the great party you had, that lasted what, four or five hours. You don't want to wake up with a financial hangover. How much value do you place on that party? Enough that you can't travel for the next few years? Can't buy the house or the car that you want? Look after your health? To what end do you want this fantasy wedding?"

BUDGETING FOR THE UNEXPECTED

We preach a good budget game, don't we? While one of us has always been a whizz with funds, the other, well, not so much. And she was devastated, and, quite frankly, too deep into the dressmaking process when she realized that her dream, custom frock would cost way more than she thought (to the tune of about $1,500 [CDN]). She ate the bill, of course, but not without some shame, and many promises (to herself and her partner) that she would find somewhere to wear it again. (She has not worn it anywhere else, btw. Sigh.)

On average, couples underestimate their wedding budget by nearly 45 percent.[92] We asked couples what some unexpected costs were that they didn't account for in their budgets. Here's what they told us (Couples' anonymity here for obvious reasons! #NoShame):

- Hair and makeup. And because I had no idea to shop around, I got worked over something awful.
- Honeymoon. I don't know how that's possible, but we literally didn't account for our honeymoon, so we went on a delayed one about six months later.

- We forgot to account for our own hotel stay for the wedding night!
- Tips! Gratuities can add up at the end of the day. For us, it was about another thousand dollars.
- Alterations cost way more than I budgeted for. Worth it, but we didn't plan for them.
- We totally forgot to budget for important ceremony stuff like the licence fee.
- Make sure you're budgeting for postage if you're mailing invitations and/or save the dates. We also fell in love with oversized invitations, which required additional (and expensive) postage.
- We didn't budget for other meals on our wedding weekend. We treated everyone to breakfast the next morning.
- We didn't count on exactly how much the photographer would cost, and we also realized late in the game that we wanted to offer transportation for our guests, so that was an added expense.
- Getting a permit for an outdoor event was annoying and the insurance was a big cost we hadn't planned for.
- My makeup artist and hair stylists all parked their cars using the hotel valet and charged it to my room.
- Vendor meals! Watch your contracts to see who you have to feed!
- I didn't plan for the costs of a new bra and underwear that worked with my dress.
- We didn't plan for champagne and snacks/brunch stuff for getting ready with the wedding party.

Planning for an extra 10 percent can help avoid any unexpected costs. Remember to add a buffer. The more time you have to plan and save, the better. While we're thinking of it, are your passports up-to-date?

Building a budget together is key for a few reasons, but mostly because it is now in both of your hands. It is shared. The expenses and planning of your wedding are shared. Everything is on the table, which will make for way less friction and unpleasant surprises than just winging it.

NEGOTIATING LIKE A BOSS

When you are starting to find all the "things" to make your wedding come together (a venue, music, floral arrangements, food, photography), keep your cards close to your chest. When calling around and getting a feel for vendors, don't ask about weddings and bridal accoutrement. Instead, put some brass in your voice and ask for quotes for a party that you're planning. Give them all the details they could ever need (date, time of day, number of guests, and menu), but withhold the tiny, incidental detail that it is a wedding until you have an estimate in hand. It gives you an excellent place from which to begin negotiations, if the price goes up. And remember, an estimate is a starting place for negotiations and there is often flexibility. Some costs, of course, are fixed, but many aren't.

For any negotiating newbie, it can be quite daunting to start the process, especially if the first time you're flexing those muscles is your wedding! Whether you have sharp negotiation skills, trying to put those to use for something as sensitive as a wedding can also throw you off. "One of the ways to get power is to ask really great questions," recommends Fotini Iconomopoulos, negotiation expert. "Ask them about their process, ask them about how much time and energy goes into something, ask them why the costs are what they are, and maybe there's some way that they can find some savings for you and them."

"If you're looking for an arrangement of flowers, for example," she continues, "and it is very hard to find that type of flower, find something that's more in season or find something that's not going to require X amount of time to make your arrangements. Is there something that you can do or source or is there energy that you can put into it that would save them time and energy?" Don't be afraid to dig deep in the name of cost savings.

Put your researcher's cap on. Iconomopoulos indicates this may be the most important tool in your toolbelt when going through negotiations. "I tell people to prepare. Know what you're getting into, know who you're dealing with, know what kind of reviews they have, know how busy they are." She suggests looking online, where you can likely find a wealth of information, but also don't be afraid to ask someone who has used their service before, as well. "Oftentimes people will tell you things like, 'Book now before that time is gone.' But do you really know if they're that busy, or are they just somebody who said that? Are they feeding you a line or is it the truth? Those are things that you want to make sure you ask around, not just depending on Google."

Iconomopoulos advises to always ask for references. "Those resources are going to be even more important than Google. I just think that doing your homework, understanding what the competitors are doing, even. You might have your sights set on one particular vendor, but what is their competition doing? How can you compare them to the competition? Why would they be charging more or less than the competition? Those are things that you also want to be thinking about."

PLANNING FOR THE UNPLANNED

Aside from sticking your nose into someone's business, literally, Iconomopoulos also recommends having a contingency plan in place, because no one wants to have to deal with rain on their wedding day, a band that didn't show up for the party, or a pandemic that prevents gatherings of more than 50 people. "I hear about so many disasters because there was an emergency. If you are signing a contract with somebody, then what can you have as a backup plan and how can you make them involved in the backup plan?"

For example, if your flowers don't come through and you don't get confirmation two days before the wedding (eeks!) that they'll be delivered, can you negotiate to get a 50 percent discount or then get out of the contract altogether? Iconomopoulos also suggests that, when negotiating with the photographer, make sure that the proofs will be delivered within X amount of days after the wedding, and if not, then you get our money back. It's those little things that Iconomopoulos doesn't want you to overlook.

"If you've heard enough horror stories and you can foresee some of those things happening, build it into the contract upfront," she says. "If they're reluctant to sign that kind of stuff, that should be a red flag in terms of how much you should trust them. If they're going, 'Yeah, of course,' then they do probably have a lot of integrity and they're willing to stand behind it."

Iconomopoulos warns against being too unreasonable in any requests (ahem, Bridezilla's need not apply), and suggests thinking more along the lines of preventing something that might happen that is out of your control.

MAKING HARD DECISIONS

Is it easy to get swept up in the planning and overspend? Yes. But at the end of the day, it is your budget and your money. "It is always your responsibility as a consumer to shop around, compare prices, and negotiate. You vote with your dollars," says finance writer Melissa Leong.[93] "If you feel like a company is taking advantage of you because you're celebrating your marriage, go with another company."

Leong and her now-husband made hard decisions on their priorities for their wedding. "It is one day. I wanted a marriage. Not a wedding. I tried to keep that in mind. I started with a blank slate and I think when you have no expectations, you are less likely to be disappointed. I just wanted a beautiful venue and amazing food and we allocated my resources there and cut everywhere else."

Their wedding ended up being at a gorgeous downtown hotel that was historically one of the first banks in Toronto, so it had resonance with Melissa as a money expert. Her husband ruthlessly negotiated when it came to the reception and they scored all of the extras — lobster and steak dinner (which her husband dubbed "lobeefster") for the price of the chicken dinner.

FIVE TIPS TO MINIMIZE FINANCIAL STRESS

1. You guessed it. The number-one tip is starting a budget. (Don't worry, more on that later — we've got you covered.) And if you are trying to ascertain what that budget should be, assume you're picking up the tab for the entire shebang. If parents offer to chip in, try to be diplomatically clear on just what they have in mind. They might offer to pick up the tab for your flowers for example, but you might be thinking that's a $2,000 bill, while they think that's a $500 bill. Either way, build a budget with the expectation that you're paying for the entire thing.

2. If you haven't already, you'll learn to master the power of negotiation when planning a wedding — consider it a new life skill that you'll come back to time and again. And even if the numbers all add up on your spreadsheet, make sure you pad your budget by 10 percent, in case there are unforeseen expenses that you don't think about, or a vendor goes rogue and there's a hidden fee you didn't anticipate.

3. Get over yourself and get over the anxiety of talking dollars with your boo as soon as possible. Like any good communication skill, these stressful talks take practice, so don't hesitate to actually have "the chat." We tell little ones every day that practice makes perfect; here's your chance to put that old adage to work as an adult. Are you planning on building a financial future together? Start now.

4. Be ready to go into austerity mode. Even if your wedding is a long way away, expect your cashflow to be tight until then. Some vendors are going to need deposits up front to secure the date, and everyone's going to need

to get paid sooner or later. You should be in mega–savings mode to build up your savings. Consider it great practice for the rest of your life. If you can manage to put away 15 percent of each paycheque leading up to your wedding, continue that diligence even after the wedding. It will just become your new normal.

5. Start from a place of knowing what your non-negotiables are and go from there. If flowers and photography are top priority, stack your budget so those costs are weighted accordingly. Then, save on other things or skip them altogether.

With their priorities in order (Beautiful venue, check! Amazing food, check!), they started their budgeting process with an estimate of how many people they wanted at the wedding, then multiplied it by the average cost of a wedding per person that they figured out, based on speaking with their friends (somewhere in the range of $100–$150 [CDN] per person). They made a list of all of the projected expenses: venue, food, photographer, florist, dress, jewellery, honeymoon, hair/makeup, transportation, DJ, programs, decor, favours, gifts for wedding party, etc. and also included a budget for incidentals. (For example, what if your venue doesn't have audiovisual capabilities and your DJ has to rent additional equipment?)

"Look at your detailed budget and set priorities. What can you sacrifice? If you want to add something, you must subtract from elsewhere. It's all about choices," Leong cautions. "Because I devoted my resources to the venue and food, I had to make sacrifices everywhere else. I got married on a Friday and in the off-season to be able to afford the venue I wanted. I bought my dress online, second hand. My bridesmaids went to Costco the morning of the wedding and made their own bouquets.

We then used those bouquets to decorate the head table," she shares. She and her now-husband also called in every favour in the universe: "My friends offered everything from photography to dance performances to desserts. It was my (affordable) dream wedding."

We know, we know, this is a wedding planning book and we're getting preachy about budgeting, but this stuff matters way more than your decor, how you look, or the other stuff that sucks up the time, energy, and ink of wedding planning.

According to a survey from BMO Financial Group, Canadian couples dip into their savings and investments to front more than half (60 percent) of their wedding costs.[94] For most North American couples, it is almost accepted that getting married is going to end in a sizable debt and some serious financial stress. Does that have to be the case?

Say it with us now: *It is not worth it.* No wedding is worth stress breakouts, zero sex drive, fighting with your partner, or going into debt over. The Institute for Divorce Financial Analysts reports that money issues are one of the three leading causes of divorce in North America. So while you might feel like it is totally worth it to max out your credit card, borrow money, or talk yourself into going over budget in order to have The Perfect Wedding, it isn't.

Weddings are never going away, but they will continue to change, notes event designer and planner Alison Slight. "Weddings are recession-proof because people will always get married, somehow, some way. They evolve, but they will never disappear. When weddings are done really specially, they are truly beautiful. My favourite part is the couple saying their vows and watching their families look on with pride. Sure, the decor can be nice, the food can be great, and the music can be good, but that's not what weddings are truly about."

Real-Life Wedding Stories

K and M found a compromise between OTT and just right.

"We were torn about whether to have a wedding at all. We live in a really expensive city and are trying to buy a house in an expensive market. That was compounded by the fact that we wanted to finance the wedding ourselves. On the other hand, we knew it was really a once-in-a-lifetime chance to celebrate and say thank you to the people we love.

"Over-the-top is just not us. We couldn't imagine having our wedding in a grand hotel ballroom surrounded by flowers. We landed on getting married up north. I grew up at our family's cottage and he grew up camping. We wanted to share the Muskokas and didn't want people to spend an arm and a leg to be at our wedding. Moreover, the most important thing was that we wanted people to be able to relax and have fun. Enter the camp idea.

"One hundred fifty-five people came up. The focus was on making people feel comfortable. Most people stayed in cabins at the camp, though our parents were quite wary of the idea of our guests sleeping in bunk beds at first; however, after the weekend they loved it! We also arranged some hotels nearby for guests that weren't into the camp (i.e., those of a certain age or pregnant).

"Our wedding was NOT turnkey. It was difficult because the space is simply not set up for weddings. It's a camp, for Pete's sake. We had to make decisions and think through every possible logistic. But my partner was very involved; we made decisions together.

"At the core was wanting to spend more time with our guests and wanting people to have fun and relax. I'm a pretty organized type A. I'm great with details and I like planning events. My mom has experience in event planning and has taught it at the college level as well, so I definitely had some support, but I found myself really caring, genuinely caring, that people were set up to have a great time, especially since we were asking them to spend an entire weekend.

"Despite me being into the details and having support from my event-planning mom, we did decide to use wedding planners. We found them on Instagram. They were building their portfolio, so we took a bit of a risk, but it was great value. The space needed very little in the way of decorations; we let the space be itself. We didn't want it over-the-top with flowers or balloons. We stuck to that simplicity and, oh boy, were we ever tested. We had to continually stick to our vision and just say no. That meant very few flowers, no guest favours, and we opted for evites to save paper and money.

"When it came to the actual wedding weekend, we mostly encouraged guests to just hang out like they would any other weekend up north at a cottage. There were options to play classic camp games and we pointed out activities like hiking trails, but we fully expected guests to just relax however they wanted. Meals were very low-key buffets.

"I found our wedding to be this great sort of return to the community wedding. Everyone pitched in where they could and it not only made it feel like a true friends and family affair, it made our wedding totally unique because it couldn't ever be replicated.

"I spoke at my wedding, something that is not traditionally encouraged of brides. We both spoke separately, but it was important to me to use the opportunity to talk to loved ones. It was very important for me to speak, for myself. I didn't want my husband to speak on my behalf. We both really wanted to tell a story, and for me, that story was that growing up as an only child, I might have lacked siblings, but all of my 'family' were in the room.

"Looking back, I hope people say that our wedding was a memorable, laid-back weekend where they felt like they were kids again at a camp, and I hope they enjoyed the beauty of the natural surroundings. I genuinely think people had fun. We definitely had a blast. We made fun of ourselves the whole time, we didn't take ourselves too seriously, and we got to spend genuine time with people."

.

8 Budgeting
You Can Make
It Work

As you read on, know that however intrepid you are, you are up against the behemoth wedding machine. Weddings are big, big business and there is a massive industry that is gaining from perpetuating the assumption that people (for the most part, women) want The Perfect Wedding. Let's get down to it. These are things that are worthy of your attention (Note: not worthy of *stress*, but worthy of your attention):

- Avoiding draining your savings or going into outrageous debt to pay for your wedding.
- Finding a nice place to get hitched and to celebrate (that fits as many

people as you'd like to invite, including those who cannot climb stairs, if that's a consideration).

- Selecting delicious food and perhaps something with which to wash it down.
- Getting a marriage licence and choosing a person to marry you, with whom you feel a reasonable connection.
- Each having an outfit in which to say "I do."
- Arranging for a photographer, because, really, a few decades later, all you're going to have to show the grandkids are photos.
- Having a stack of thank-you notes to send after the wedding.

These are things that don't matter so much:

- What other people wear to the wedding (your wedding party, your mom, your in-laws, none of it matters).
- Hosting a rehearsal dinner (you can certainly have a rehearsal without a dinner, if a rehearsal is needed at all).
- Whether you register for china or silver or even a toaster.
- If your invitations are raised print or even printed at all.
- Having a colour scheme for your wedding.
- Artfully placing mason jars throughout the venue.
- Being "perfect."

BREAKING THINGS INTO BUDGETS

These are just sample budgets; you gotta figure out your own priorities.

Budget Items

For your wedding budget, account for:

- Reception (venue rental, food, and bar): approx. 50%
- Ceremony/officiant and marriage licence: approx. 3%
- Attire: approx. 6%

- Flowers and decor: approx. 6%
- Entertainment/music: approx. 8%
- Photography/videography: approx. 10%
- Stationery: approx. 2%
- Wedding rings: approx. 2%
- Parking/transportation (for the couple): approx. 1%
- Gifts for your friends and/or attendants: approx. 2%
- Unexpected costs: 10%

Here are some sample scenarios for how this math plays out:

Spending Between $5,000 and $6,000 (CDN)

Let's say you want to get married in eight months; without any prior savings you would need to start saving about $375 each paycheque in order to save about $5,600. If that amount per paycheque is too high, which it damn well might be, you'll need to adjust your wedding expectations accordingly.

Think of the number of guests you'd like to have (remember our early planning advice?) and look at how far that budget will carry you. Can you host 80 people for $2,500 (CDN), which is about half of your savings? You sure can, though it means finding a cheap venue and keeping your food and beverage costs on the light side. Hosting a brunch or afternoon tea is going to be more affordable than an evening reception (one major factor in keeping costs down is that less alcohol is typically consumed during the day than at night). You can also make your budget work hard by enlisting the help of family and friends. Save your budget for making the experience feel special, so rather than pay for catering to make and serve food, get family and friends to make or source the food and set up food stations, then pay for dish rentals and a few people to staff the reception by clearing plates and topping up the food stations. Why plate rentals? They pick up the dishes unwashed, so it is money well spent. For food, think heaps of gorgeous croissants,

HOW MUCH WINE DO I REALLY NEED?

A bottle of wine (750 mL) yields six four-ounce glasses. You can plan for your guests to drink about an average of two glasses of wine per hour, less as the night goes on. So check this out: If you are hosting 150 guests for an hour cocktail party then dinner and dancing after (so four hours), you'd want to plan for 300 glasses of wine for your cocktail hour and another 750 or so glasses for the rest of the night. Some guests will drink more, and some will drink less, so it will balance itself out. This works out to 175 bottles of wine, or 15 cases. Listen: the odds of your guests drinking more than a bottle of wine each are slim, but best to err on the side of caution lest you run out. If you're serving beer or cocktails, roll back your wine, unless your friends are animals. Also worth noting, if you purchase the booze under your own event permit, go over a bit to make sure everyone is taken care of alcohol-wise. Better over a bit than under. And if everything is under your permit, you can likely take back any unopened bottles for a refund. If your venue is ordering your alcohol, confirm that you'll only be charged for what is poured.

quiches, and tarts. If you are trying to stretch every dollar but still want a few nice flourishes, serve a Prosecco or sparkling wine cocktail. You'll go through fewer bottles if it's served two-parts sparkling wine to one-part raspberry soda, for example. Plus, if you are serving it in a cocktail, you can buy a lower-end bottle since the flavour is going to be blended, anyway.

Sample Budget

- Reception (rental, food, and bar): approx. $3,000
- Ceremony/officiant and marriage licence: approx. $250
- Attire: approx. $450
- Flowers and decor: approx. $400
- Entertainment/music: approx. $450
- Photography/videography: approx. $500
- Stationery: approx. $200
- Wedding rings: approx. $150 for each ring, $300
- Parking/transportation (for the couple): about $50
- Gifts for your friends and/or attendants: approx. $150 total
- Unexpected costs: $500–$600

Spending Between $10,000 and $12,000 (CDN)

Start saving. If your wedding is a year away, aim to save $1,000 each month to pad your budget. In one year, you will have saved $12,000. Here's how a wedding budget could shake out: When you're looking at hosting a party for $5,000 (with reception costs tallying about half of your savings for the wedding), consider the time of day. At an evening event, most people consume three drinks. If you have 100 guests, you can safely estimate a bottle of wine for every two guests: 50 bottles of wine at $40 each (look out for those markups and corkage fees). Your bar costs could be about $2,000, which leaves about $3,000 for food and venue. Totally doable. Keep your food costs down by first setting a cost-per-head that you need to stick to, rather than select a predetermined menu from a caterer. Watch out for markups and instead ask for them to come up with some options for $20 (or $15, or $35, whatever you land on) per person.

Hosting your ceremony and reception in the same place can net some cost savings and you would save on decor, too. If you get sticker shock from the price of flowers (join the club), opt for just one or two really bold arrangements. Pack the rest of the space with white candles. Find them for cheap on Kijiji or a craft or dollar store and set them out in groups on mirrors. Voilà. Super romantic. Sell them online or give them to another couple getting married for extra-good wedding karma.

Sample Budget

- Reception (rental, food, and bar): approx. $5,000
- Ceremony/officiant and marriage licence: approx. $300
- Attire: approx. $800
- Flowers and decor: approx. $800
- Entertainment/music: approx. $800
- Photography/videography: approx. $1,000
- Stationery: approx. $200
- Wedding rings: approx. $150 for each ring, $300
- Parking/transportation (for the couple): approx. $100
- Gifts for your friends and/or attendants: approx. $200
- Unexpected costs: $1,000 to $1,200

Spending Between $25,000 and $30,000 (CDN)

Here's the thing about wanting to spend $25,000 on a wedding: You're in an echelon of events where it's really easy to get swept up into spending $35,000 or $40,000. Prepare thyself for an onslaught of upsells. Planning to spend $6,000 on your food for the night? For an extra $3,000 you can have an oyster station! That sort of shit a) adds up fast, and b) won't make or break your wedding. Go back to your list of absolute deal-breakers and use them as your north star. Late-night food service has become a common upsell and, most of the time, the food doesn't get eaten — you know your guests better than your caterer does, so it's up to you.

Factor in how much the actual venue fee is versus food and bar. Buying out a restaurant for an evening might seem extravagant, but if

FIVE SUPER EASY WAYS TO SAVE

1. Prioritize three things that matter the most. Identify three things that are really important to you as a couple. Maybe it is the catering because you love food, a great band to dance the night away to, and a photographer whose work you love. Shop around for those items first so the rest of your budget can fall in line.

2. Have a smaller wedding. It sounds harsh but it is really simple: invite fewer people to your wedding and your costs will go down.

3. Ask your vendors for their advice. People seem shy about asking their vendors if they have any advice to trim their budget. Put on your adult pants and do it!

4. Cut your stationery. Is having that oversized square envelope that requires double the postage really worth it? Do you need printed invitations at all?

5. Skip the limo. They're expensive and sort of a prom throwback. Roll up in an Uber black car or take a taxi.

you only have to hit a certain food and beverage minimum for them to throw in the actual space for free, that can be a totally turnkey, easy option. If you want some extra touches for your ceremony, your budget could support having a cellist or something, if that's your jam.

You can scale up on your photography if you like, but focus on the quality of the photographer rather than buying a prefab package with a certain number of photos. Any good photographer is going to give you unmarked shots, anyway.

Sample Budget

- Reception (rental, food, and bar): approx. $12,500
- Ceremony/officiant and marriage licence: approx. $800
- Attire: approx. $2,250
- Flowers and decor: approx. $2,250
- Entertainment/music: approx. $2,250
- Photography/videography: approx. $2,750
- Stationery: approx. $625
- Wedding rings: approx. $625
- Parking/transportation (for the couple): approx. $250
- Gifts: approx. $625
- Unexpected costs: $2,500

You get the idea. The big takeaway here is to save well in advance of the wedding (with the caveat that you're going to need to manage your cash flow and write some cheques well before the actual wedding date), set a final budget, and prioritize what matters most to you within that budget. Once you have a template for a budget, pad it by about 10 percent.

BUDGETING BREAKDOWNS

Choosing Your Venue

The most obvious places to get married are likely going to have standard packages. Think event halls and hotels. While fairly turnkey, weddings in venues like this are likely pretty cookie cutter — with cookie-cutter budget packages, too. The benefit is that everything is done for you, so you're working from their shortlist of options, but the risk is that you're limited to their list and their costs. What if their preferred vendors are a fortune? Or you love the venue, but the food and bar options are sky high?

There is the option to go more à la carte and cherry-pick every element of your wedding. You might be able to find a venue for a song but

INDOOR OR OUTDOOR VENUE CONSIDERATIONS

Debating whether to opt for an indoor or outdoor venue? Consider the following:

Indoor spaces are going to be a bit more turnkey, as they'll likely have the basics (like tables, chairs, and dishware) covered. Indoor spaces will likely include a kitchen or at least something close to one. An outdoor venue can be a gorgeous blank slate, though it might require all of these conveniences to be brought in. You'll also need to make a rain plan. Consider renting a tent, flooring, and heaters, if the weather calls for it. And washrooms: ensure your guests have access to an abundance of washrooms!

have to budget to bring in a tent or rentals. Don't be intimidated by this route. It opens up a myriad of new venue options and potentially some savings. Think about historic buildings in your city, and restaurants as well as museums, galleries, and botanical gardens. Some are full of character and surprisingly affordable.

Beyond the actual place you get married, time of year affects your budget, too. Saturday nights are often the most popular time to host any party, so the costs reflect that. But what about a Friday night? Or a swank Sunday afternoon affair?

Go through your venue with a fine-tooth comb. If you see a "ceremony fee" in your venue estimate, ask if there is room to negotiate it, or to have it waived. Ensure that you're not on the hook for anything else. Is gratuity included or is that additional? Are you responsible for leaving the venue in "swept condition" after the party winds down? Sharpen those negotiation skills, and don't make any assumptions (ahem, read the fine print).

Choosing Your Flowers and Decor

There's no denying that fresh flowers are one of life's true pleasures, but damned if they aren't a fortune. Florals can take a serious bite out of your budget, when you factor in bouquets (if you're into that), plus blooms for the ceremony and the reception. Josh Spiegel, creative director at NY-based Birch Event Design, cautions that there is so much subjectivity. "A lush white rose ball might be $50 from the bride's perspective, the florist down the road might be $100 and mine is $400. Yet, we think we're all talking about the same thing, using the same terminology." It is time well spent to ensure you and your florist (well, any vendor you're working with) are on the same page.

If you're looking to save some dough, perhaps look to who gets flowers on the day of your wedding. Carrie Fisher of Roadside Florist says to consider the number in your wedding party — the lower the number, the lower the amount you need to spend on flowers. "If you have 10 bridesmaids that adds up," says Fisher. "The whole idea of having boutonnieres and corsages for everyone — grandparents, parents — adds up and maybe isn't that necessary. It is a nice touch and someone's nana would really appreciate a corsage, but if you're on a budget, maybe she doesn't need one. A flower girl [may come with] a flower crown or the basket of petals and she's one year old. That's $100 (CDN) that maybe you didn't need to spend." Also, look at flowers that are still pretty, but are not the hottest thing in weddings, suggests Fisher. As popularity goes up, so does pricing, because of supply and demand.

Doing your own florals is super-duper easy, if you're into it, like our couple Cody and Turner AhTave. They stayed up late the night before the wedding putting together flower arrangements with their family and wedding party. "We didn't want anyone to feel like they were working, but we did want to bring our friends along for the journey in ways that felt meaningful," says Cody. Hit up some YouTube videos, get some floral wire and dollar-store glassware. Befriend a local flower market to find out what's local, cheap, and plentiful at that time of year. Importing peonies when they are out of season can cost five times more per stem than something that is local and more easily available. Instead of trying to Martha Stewart it, go monochromatic with a ton of the same blooms or by keeping it all in the same colour family. Fill out your florals with lots and lots of greenery. By upping the ratio of greenery, you can lighten up on the number of flowers you have to buy, with big savings. And keep your ambitions within your talent. Now might not be the time to attempt a five-foot installation to be suspended from the ceiling.

There is life beyond flowers, too. A bunch of friends have something we've dubbed the Sisterhood of the Travelling Candles. Bride #1 bought a metric ton of white pillar candles and amazing hurricane vases. Bride #2 got married a few months later and asked Bride #1 what she did with all of her decor. She bought them for a reasonable rate, and so did Bride #3 and so on. Pillar candles take forever to burn, so three weddings later, they still looked stunning. Cover any area in enough white candles and it will look super romantic. If you want to doll it up even more, arrange clusters of white candles (doesn't matter the shape, size or container) on top of mirrors. It looks fancy. Trust.

Choosing Your Food and Bar

When you're planning what to serve for the night, think beyond what is presented to you as an option. Not to be crass, but the people presenting you these options are making a buck on your wedding, so the options they give you are most likely the exact same thing sent to any other couple sussing out wedding menus. Ask what other dishes they could suggest and shop around judiciously.

When it comes to your food menu, a tried-and-true trick is to go light on the light stuff and heavy on the heavier offerings. A beautiful bite of tuna on a cucumber square looks stunning but will be far more expensive and less filling than, say, crab cakes. Carb it up for a more substantial menu that's also a bit lighter on your wallet.

Hot Tip: Don't Be So Quick to Clear Away Those Glasses

Yes, you want to avoid a sea of dishes and glasses piling up, but some serving staff are WAY too quick to clear a glass of wine that someone has had three sips from. Someone might have just popped over to say hi to a friend and when they return, will likely head to the bar to get a new glass of wine. That makes for a lot of waste (and an unnecessarily large bar bill). Don't get all obsessed about it, but if you feel like mentioning to your venue manager/catering person, whomever, it might save some waste.

If you are planning canapés, assume that you'll need three to four per person, per hour, if that is all you are serving. If you are having a cocktail hour or a few hors d'oeuvres before dinner, you can scale back and plan for a few per person, per hour. Consider adding a few food stations if you aren't serving passed hors d'oeuvres. Put them on opposite sides of the room to keep guests from crowding into one area. Dips and crudités could also be an economical option here.

Bar packages can be pricey and depending on how much your crowd consumes, paying per pour might be far more economical. Look at the possibility of bringing in your own wine — even with a corkage fee factored in, there might be some serious savings. Another added bonus to bringing your own alcohol is that typically any unopened bottles can be returned (but check the return policy first, obviously). Ask that no shots be poured that night because a) they'll quickly make your bar costs rocket up, and b) shots turn people into hooligans.

If you're doing a champagne toast, instruct staff to only pour a half a glass of bubbly into everyone's flute. Most people will only take a sip or two to toast you anyway, then ditch that glass for their preferred drink. If you have 150 guests and conservatively order 24 bottles for a toast, you could realistically get by with ordering only 12 bottles, and maybe a few to spare just in case.

You can also help keep bar costs down by closing the bar during dinner service or even a half hour before your reception ends. In fact, your special-occasion permit might even require that you shut down your bar service before your party officially ends. Read that fine print!

Don't have a cash bar. Just don't. You are likely thinking, "Hold up, isn't the whole premise of this book to empower me to do things how we want to?" Yes. But inviting people to your wedding then asking them to pay for their own glass of wine is — how do we say this delicately? — going to get people talking. And they will likely talk about it for years. Trust us. Do not have a cash bar.

Who says you need to have a cocktail hour before dinner? Your entire wedding reception can be one gorgeous cocktail party with no sit-down dinner. One couple served dinner buffet-style, pulling in food from multiple local restaurants that they loved. It can also be a beautiful family style dinner on long, stunningly decorated tables with no cocktail party.

Lastly, and perhaps most importantly, you don't want people smashed at your wedding. You do not want people sloppy, fall-down drunk, or worse, driving drunk. So, while it is great to keep your bar costs down, the more important priority is for everyone to have a great time and get home safely.

Being Smart About Your Photography

Book a photographer, but not necessarily a wedding photographer. When you think about the super cheesy wedding photos that grace most mantles, that's what most wedding photographers specialize in: portrait shots. Any good editorial or journalistic photographer worth their salt is going to know how to capture the emotion in the moment — which is the really good, juicy stuff. Look in local newspapers and magazines for the names of photographers, or search photographers in your area. Don't book someone based on what their website looks like — that means that they have a great website person, not necessarily amazing photography skills.

Once you've found a few photographers that you like, narrow it down to three or four and go meet with them.

HERE IS THE MOST DEFINITIVE LIST OF QUESTIONS FOR FINDING THE PHOTOGRAPHER OF YOUR DREAMS

What other photography do you shoot?
Do they shoot events or editorial? Can they show you examples of their wedding and non-wedding work? Look at work done in different settings, times of year, and vibes. If you see three dozen versions of the same posed photo with the same black-and-white treatment, keep looking. Unless, that's umm, your thing. Ask about portraits versus candids, as you'll likely want a nice mix of both.

Do you sell photography packages or shoot hourly?
Some photographers will sell packages that include a certain number of printed photos (remember your school photos as a kid? Yeah, like that) or an album. Others will simply give you a USB or site to download your photos (which we love, so you can print them off forever and ever for cheap).

What will I actually get after the wedding?
How many photos can you expect, 50 or 500? Are proofs watermarked or unmarked? Are any photos edited or retouched? If they do retouching, to what degree and on how many photos? Side question: Are you sure you want retouched images? If they are providing you with prints, ensure they are on the good stuff: Acid-free, archival-quality photo paper.

Will you work from a shot list?
A shot list is basically your wish list of photos, sort of like a checklist. If they are open to it, it can be very helpful so that you get the photos that you'll be really bummed if they were missed (like one shot with both your parents

for example, or you mom with all her sisters, you get the idea). When you're on the subject, ask if they are familiar with where they'll be shooting or if they'd like to see the space in advance.

Do you shoot just digital or film, too?
Digital is ubiquitous, but film is sort of cool again. You want to ask because, while film has sort of a dreamy, ethereal quality, it doesn't work in every space. Also, this is where things get ridiculous: Choosing a film photographer doesn't necessarily mean that you'll only get prints. Some photographers develop their film, scan the images, then create high-resolution digital files. Sounds exhausting. And cool.

What exactly is included in your rate?
Try to get a sense of not only how many hours, but the number and type of photos you can expect. Ask about transportation, post-production or editing costs, shipping, overtime, do you need to feed them? Ask about everything.

How many hours do YOU recommend, and at what stage of the day?
Be strategic with which hours you book for, and you might decide you don't need them for as long as you think you do. #BudgetSavings.

What is the payment schedule and total fee?
Ask about every damn detail on how much you are paying them and when.

Who is *actually* holding the camera?
If you are going through the exercise of finding a photographer that you click with, then for heaven's sake, you

want them (not their assistant) to come photograph your wedding. Ask if they are coming themselves, and if they are bringing an assistant. Be sure to ask what their plan is if they are sick. It happens.

What can we expect for the day?
Will they have a camera an inch from your face when you're saying your vows? Will they show up with a huge lighting kit? Are they planning on bringing you to shoot offsite? If so, ask where, why, and how you're all planning to get there and back. Will they wear jeans and flip flops? Leave nothing to chance.

Don't ask about wedding packages. Instead, ask about their rate for however many hours you need them. Be clear about asking for all unmarked photos digitally within a week or so. A heads-up: If you want any digital retouching or editing, it will cost more and take longer.

Ask to see their work and make sure you like them — they're going to be stuck like glue to you and your beloved for an entire day. Fit is crucial. There is something undeniably intimate about someone taking your picture all day. Editorial photographer Kayla Rocca never accepts a job without speaking with the couple to ensure they are a fit. "You're with photographers for the entire day, so you want to make sure that you connect with that photographer and the photographer wants to make sure that they connect with the couple. Both of their ideas need to be aligned, because there are so many types of photographers out there, and so many types of couples. You want to make sure that you're a match."

Rocca caps the number of weddings she shoots a year at 15. "Wedding photography is pretty physically demanding. You're on your feet ten to twelve hours a day and you're lugging all your

KAREN HIRED THE BIGGEST JERK OF A PHOTOGRAPHER

I called a photographer to enquire about rates and availability to shoot a party on a Saturday night from 8 p.m. to midnight. The photographer got all the details they needed: About 50 guests, natural lighting, only candid shots, and would like digital files of unmarked proofs in about a week. The photographer came back with a reasonable rate, about $1,000 (CDN). I said, "Awesome, let's book it!"

The weeks ticked by and, closer to the wedding, I touched base with them. She assured me that everything is great. "Out of curiosity," asked the photographer, "what exactly is the event I'm shooting?" "Oh, it's my wedding," I explained. The photographer literally tripled their rate, on the spot.

I politely enquired how it changed the quote. Are the hours, equipment, and deliverables any different? The photographer awkwardly stumbled and landed on a lousy "Because, weddings, they just are." I told her that her services are no longer needed, in a decidedly less polite way. Perhaps with a gratuitous cuss.

I looked at the photographer credits in the local newspaper and found a few photojournalist photographers and tracked them down on LinkedIn. I clicked with one and his rates were totally reasonable. Our photos are stunning. He got candid shots like only a photojournalist can.

equipment and gear, and you have two cameras with you and you're constantly shooting. You're observing everything that's going on and you're taking the photo, directing, framing. It's a lot of work. On top of that there's editing of the images, which takes a long time, trying to curate the pictures for your couple." Having a well-rounded photographer compared to a photographer who shoots only weddings can be hugely underrated. They're going to have a more diverse skill set and that often produces better photos.

Planning Your Music

Like the food, people remember whether the music was any good at a wedding. Whether you have a band, a DJ, or whip up your own playlist depends on the type of wedding you're after, your venue, and your budget. Bands, while typically more expensive, sort of function like entertainment and can make an occasion feel grand. A DJ should be able to play to your crowd and get people on the dance floor, if that's your jam. If you're going for a low-key, more cocktail-party vibe, you could get a small band or do a playlist yourself with music that increases in energy. If you're going the DIY route, test the sound system at the venue yourself with the actual device and playlist. Don't leave anything to chance. Fade your songs together so you don't leave weird pauses in between songs, obv.

Questions to Ask Your Band or DJ

- Do they have a go-to playlist? If so, can you see it?
- Can they include a few songs at your request?
- Will they take requests that night?
- Could the singer (if you're having a band) also double as an emcee?
- Are they familiar with your venue? If not, do they want a site visit?
- How many hours do they cover? Do they take a break at midnight?
- Should you plan to feed them?

- Do they bring any signage? (If they say yes, ask them not to … it looks tacky.)
- What A.V. equipment they will come with, and what will you need to rent? You don't want to have to go searching for some random cable or wire while your guests are rolling in.
- There are songs that turn people into absolute animals at weddings. You might think that no wedding reception is complete without "YMCA," "Mony Mony," and the "Chicken Dance." You do you.

HIRING A WEDDING COORDINATOR

Wedding coordinators can be total rock stars that shield you from dealing with some pretty tedious things. But they can also cost a pretty penny. Coordinators can cost around 15 to 18 percent of your budget, or some may offer a flat rate of $5,000 (CDN) to $10,000 (CDN), and this is likely on top of your actual budget, though it's worth noting that wedding coordinators do have relationships with vendors, so they will likely be able to save you money in other areas of the budget. You'll need to shop around, of course, to find the right coordinator fit.

If you find planning events totally overwhelming and really just want to leave it to a pro, wedding planners can be worth their weight in gold. Like, literally. Because they're so hooked up in the industry, they can often negotiate some great deals on your behalf. If you're marrying in a venue that hosts a lot of weddings, there might be an onsite wedding coordinator who will be your point person, as well as ensuring things run smoothly on the big day.

There are also independent wedding planners. Ask for recommendations and meet with a few to find one that you really click with. They should have experience, a great eye for style, be professional, and you should genuinely like being around them. Some will work for a flat fee; others will work from a percentage of your budget.

If you are getting married in a city that you don't live in, a wedding coordinator might be a sage decision. A wedding coordinator, in general, will be able to

- take your ideas and bring them to life;
- help with setting up a budget and sticking to it;
- narrow down your venues and reserve the date;
- find and book all of your suppliers, and ensure they all get paid;
- create a detailed hour-by-hour rundown of the wedding day (you should do one for yourself, by the way, whether or not you have a wedding coordinator);
- arrange any rentals that need to be brought in and taken out; and
- be the go-to on the big day, troubleshooting, answering questions, or advising as needed.

Acknowledging Where Wedding Coordinators Can Save You, Literally and Emotionally

Alison Slight is one half of the luxury event design and production company Candice & Alison Events group (so, literally an expert in all things events). "I can speak to our wedding clientele and say that they all have two things in common among them: The first is that they come to us because they don't have the time to plan a wedding. The second is that they have high-pressure lives." While there is an old-school mentality that persists, that notion that you're only going to do it once (ahem, we know that is not always the case), so spend the time and money to do it right, Slight maintains that there are actually two schools of thought. That classic go-big-or-go-home mindset, or this other way of thinking that is do it beautifully, but do it super simple and save for a home and/or your future.

If you're marrying later than your friends, odds are you've attended enough weddings to get a sense of what you like or don't like. If that's not the case it can feel very overwhelming. And the wedding industry can sometimes prey upon that. "People are constantly trying to upsell couples. We're so cautious of this and protect our clients from that pressure," says Slight. "We alleviate that stress but there are people who capitalize on it."

Essentially, check in with how you're feeling when looking for a wedding planner. Do you feel like your needs are being met without any pressure to spend, spend, spend? If yes, then you're in the right place.

Being Your Own Wedding Coordinator

If you opt to plan your own wedding, it is still a good idea to find or appoint someone your coordinator for your wedding day. Someone needs to have a full list of all the suppliers dropping things off that day and what time they're slated to arrive (and that "someone" doesn't necessarily have to be you). You know the friend who is über-organized and makes notes using colour-coded markers and highlighters? Ask them to help. Seriously.

Find a solid, trustworthy friend and ask if they can take on the role of making sure the day runs smoothly (see the section on wedding party tasks in Chapter 9). You can also ask your venue how much support they can lend in this area, but please, don't try to be baking and decorating your wedding cake, arranging flowers, and testing your audio while attempting liquid eyeliner for the first time on your wedding day.

DESTINATION WEDDINGS

You might be thinking that destination weddings are cheaper and easier, but that's not necessarily true. Things to consider about a destination wedding:

It will likely be smaller. Realistically, fewer people can come to a destination wedding. Between the travel costs and time off work, you'll likely end up with a smaller guest list than if you got married in your

PAYING FOR YOUR WEDDING PARTY'S TRAVEL

When you ask someone to be in your wedding party for a destination wedding, be super clear about what costs you expect them to cover, versus which costs you'll take on. You could say something to the effect of, "So we landed on Aruba for the wedding, five days in late January. If you can get yourself down there, I'd be over the moon for you to be my maid of honour. We have the hotel and meals covered."

There aren't hard-and-fast rules about who covers which costs for a destination wedding, so if there is someone who you desperately want to come to your wedding, but they can't afford it, it is really nice of you to pay for their way, if you can swing it. Just ask them to swear an oath of secrecy so that other guests don't start to wonder if you are looking after everyone's costs.

locale. What's more, travel can be tough for elderly folks and families with little kids, so take that into account for a destination wedding. A smaller wedding might be a very good or a not-so-good thing for you.

It can be very, very turnkey. Resort destination weddings are the meal kits of weddings. That shit gets shipped in a box, totally ready for you to cook. They are easy and 90 percent of the work is done for you. If you really like to get creative in the kitchen, you might find meal kits restrictive. You might LOVE the idea of just showing up at your wedding or you might find it feels like a wedding assembly line. Again, this is about you guys, so see how each one makes you feel and stick with it.

It might be a shocking amount of work. If you are planning a wedding in another place that isn't turnkey (see above), it will most likely take considerable work. You can do your best to keep things easy and simple, but at the end of the day, you are still planning a party in another place, sometimes with time zone, currency, and language differences. This might sound fun to you. This might sound like a nightmare to you.

It might be more expensive than you think. Destination weddings beget travel, and travel isn't cheap. Some couples find destinations where they can stretch their budget a bit further so they go for a smaller but more lavish wedding in a beautiful space, but in the end, they might not save a penny. If you go this route you'll likely rack up some decent long-distance charges, and you might want to go down a few days before the wedding, ship stuff in advance, pay for extra baggage, or pay for other people's travel costs (should you so choose). These costs shouldn't dissuade you from getting hitched however the hell you want, but some couples assume that destination weddings are inherently less expensive, and that isn't always the case.

It isn't a honeymoon. It might sound so smart and efficient to mash your wedding up with your honeymoon, which is what destination weddings are all about. But, dear reader, being in a beautiful setting with your loved ones is not the same as a honeymoon with just the two of you. And by honeymoon, we, of course, mean one-on-one-sex-until-you-can't-sex-no-more time. It just isn't the same with your parents, in-laws, and friends milling about.

It might be more grief to cancel. Let's just say, hypothetically, that a global health pandemic forces couples all over the world to postpone their wedding plans. The travel and accommodation costs associated with destination weddings might be difficult to cancel and recoup.

Real-Life Wedding Stories

A and L leaned on a keen family member to plan their day.

"My sister was really hoping we'd get married, and when we got engaged she immediately had a vision. I didn't have much of an idea and she had all these ideas and loves to plan a good party, so we went with it. Her home is about an hour outside of the city, so totally doable for a day trip.

"As the planning progressed, we knew we wanted everyone to feel like they were having dinner at our place — a ton of food on the buffet; very white, clean, neutral settings — we just sort of naturally knew how to make it feel like ours. Having the wedding at a family home (rather than a venue that churns out weddings like a factory line) also made it feel like 'us.'

"My now-husband and I deferred to each other for different things: I left the band and all the music selection for the night up to him. I deferred to my sister a lot.

"We all took a few days off before the wedding and did all the decorating, one element of which was hanging hundreds of paper cranes from the ceiling. It was tedious and time-consuming, but I love that we did that together.

"We have the real benefit of having two families that weren't overpowering about our wedding. We paid for half our wedding ourselves and our families paid for the rest between them. They just gave us money, without asking to help shape the wedding in any way. That was really refreshing because when it came to the guest list, things got a bit tense, but still no one tried to leverage their financial support. We opted to invite more friends than certain family members. His family sort of understood, but it didn't land so well with my family. We emailed people and said the guest list is super small, to sort of pre-emptively plant a seed that they wouldn't be receiving an invitation. It was yucky, but the right thing to do so that we could have our friends there.

"We had planned for our wedding to be outside, and on the day it was hotter than hell and there was a tornado warning — weather that just doesn't happen in our climate. Right before the guests arrived, someone said to me, 'You need to go fix your hair.' I looked in the mirror and looked like a drowned rat. I was like, 'I don't care. Let's go.' We just rolled with it. I actually cut the officiant off because it was so fucking hot outside and I wanted them to hurry up.

"After the wedding, we had all these really lovely cards from people. We don't want to be hoarders, but it felt weird to just toss these cards into the recycling. We kept them in a box and then one night a few years after the wedding, we hauled out the box and sat down and read them one at a time. We soaked up all the joy then tossed them into the fire, one by one."

9 Party Planning
Making It All Happen and Still Staying Sane

PLANNING THOSE PRE-WEDDING PARTIES

Comedian Ali Wong hit the nail on the head about being in wedding parties. When asked about her wedding on *The Ellen DeGeneres Show* (Wong got married at city hall, by the way), she had this to say: "When people would ask me, 'Do you want to be my bridesmaid?' I started to hear 'Do you want to be financially burdened? Do you want to spend $150 on this bogus-ass dress that you're never going to wear again and spend a weekend with a bunch of bitches that you don't know?' There's always some weird cousin with braces who is socially awkward and they're like, 'Here's a penis necklace, here's a penis hat. Let's play pin the penis on the penis.'"[95]

She's not wrong.

As if a wedding wasn't enough pressure or large enough undertaking, enter engagement parties, bridal teas, bachelor parties, bachelorettes, stag and doe's, and showers. Some brides relish the OTT feting and all that extra attention, while others find them completely uncomfortable.

If you fall into the first camp of the more the celebrating the better, here is a cautionary word: No one is as excited about your wedding as you are. If you're asking your friends to come to your engagement party, then to Vegas for a weekend, an afternoon shower (there is an assumption that gifts are sort of tied to these), AND your wedding, you're asking for an awful lot. And if you're thinking, "But we all do it for each other, so it is fine" — fair, but all that means is everyone's weekends are spoken for forever. Feel free to liberate your social circle by scaling back the pre-wedding events. Because even if you're on the fence about them, it is very easy to get caught up in the sequin- or dress shirt–infused whirlwind.

One recent bride lamented to us that a friend got so swept up in the pre-wedding spin that it put a wedge between them that they never fixed. "One of the first weddings I went to after university was a good friend of mine. She got *really* caught up in her wedding. I went to three showers for her (she had at least five or six by the end), and by that stage I was just over it. I watched it grow and grow and grow, and I couldn't do it anymore. I remember thinking this isn't remotely how it is supposed to be. We're not friends anymore. I don't speak to her. No question that it would have been the most over-the-top, beautiful wedding, but I couldn't bring myself to attend. It was just more more more more."

We share this cautionary tale because if you are so blessed that multiple people want to throw parties in your honour, keep an eye out for how much it is taxing the people around you — and not just the people hosting, but the people invited.

Let's say you're looking at an engagement party, bridal tea, bachelor/bachelorette, a shower (or two, if both sides of the family are feeling it), PLUS the wedding — you can scale it back. Prioritize an event (or two, or three, you get the gist) and encourage a merging of guest lists to keep things tighter.

Understanding that Weddings Are Enough

Why all the pre-game events? And when did they become so extravagant anyway?

Dr. Beth Montemurro, a professor of sociology at Penn State University, points out that over the past 15 or 20 years, as weddings have become more lavish and indulgent so have bachelorette parties.[96] An entire industry has popped up, offering bachelorette party packages or weekend getaways. Some destinations have become synonymous with the event: Las Vegas, Nashville, Atlantic City, and Cancun have all become common places to mark the last days of singlehood. We can blame social media, to some degree. Carly Gieseler, a professor of communications at the City University of New York, authored a 2017 study making the case that social media has taken things that used to be privately or intimately celebrated and made them public.[97]

The more we see these public celebrations, the more we normalize them and assume that everyone celebrates similarly. What's more, our social-media streams are our highlight reels, so you can bet that those photos make us look goooooooood. Not only does everything get documented online, it is in an extremely stylized, glamourized way. Which continually raises the pressure to do it as big, as pretty, and as grand as the next guy/gal. Gieseler asserts that it can feel impossible to escape the pressure of these once-unconventional celebrations when social media makes them feel ubiquitous.

Social media also cranks up our FOMO, appealing to our bratty ego — we want what they have, but better. It is peer pressure times 1,000. It has become pretty standard in some social circles to go all out for the marathon of additional lead-up events and the wedding. Glitzy engagement parties, bachelor and bachelorette weekends a two- or three-hour flight away, matching wedding party T-shirts/robes/swimwear, a bridal shower, a bridal tea, a rehearsal dinner … the list goes on. And on. Because we all see these events on social media, we have normalized them to the degree that we have institutionalized them: We assume this is just what we do.

It's Okay to Say No

When asked how a couple should navigate these events if they don't want to be the centre of attention or feel like they're not in line with who they are, sociologist Dr. Beth Montemurro's advice is simple: Don't do it. She shares that many of the people she's spoken to in her research aren't into bridal showers. They feel overly feminine and make people uncomfortable, particularly because of the whole ritual of opening gifts in front of other people and having to come up with original things to say. It's very awkward if you're thanking people for getting you gifts, particularly when you registered for them, so you already know what they're going to be and have to think of new ways to say thank you.

Sheila asked for no bachelorette party and no bridal shower.[98] "In the end, I had one of each," she said. "My mom said that a shower would mean a lot to my grandma and my aunts, so I went along with it. I'm way more of a behind-the-scenes girl and found it really uncomfortable to be the centre of attention. My friends were great about planning a low-key bachelorette night — I didn't want anything over-the-top. They planned a dinner that my mom and sisters could come to, then some friends and I went out after." All this is to say, keeping it simple can still be very, very meaningful.

Couples getting hitched often bemoan that all the hoopla is just to appease other people, lest they seem ungrateful. They don't want to disappoint people who want to plan an engagement party or a shower. But we're here to give you permission to have that conversation. Maybe your parents felt pressured when they got married, so they're just repeating what they went through as if there isn't any other way. Or maybe they are just super psyched and want to celebrate every part of your engagement that they can. (Who can blame them?)

Tell them if you're feeling overwhelmed by the events leading up to your wedding. If you go through your engagement and wedding (or hell, your life) swallowing your feelings to make other people happy, you'll end up super bummed out — and feeling like your emotions aren't valid. If you don't put yourself first (with a gentle but firm hand, of course), no one else will. Name a more important time to have a strong sense of self than when you merge your life with another. Stick to what feels right for you.

The Backstory of Bachelor Parties and Bridal Showers

"In wedding planning and wedding history books, there is a story that kept coming up over and over again," explains Dr. Montemurro, who researches sexual development. Her dissertation explores bachelor parties and bridal showers. The story goes like this: In 16th- or 17th-century Holland, there was a woman who wanted to marry, but the man that she wanted to marry was poor, and so her father wouldn't give permission to marry because he was concerned they didn't have what they needed. There was no dowry. Distraught, this woman's friends and family came together to create a dowry for her by putting together all the things that she needed to get married. They came to the house and dropped off items, essentially showering her with gifts. Her father finally gave permission and they got married.

If this story, passed down over centuries, is true, it certainly doesn't put bridal showers in the best light. It harkens to the materialistic and transactional elements of weddings, and the importance of a father's approval for a woman to marry. Not very romantic. And very patriarchal.

What's interesting, Montemurro explains, is that it wasn't until the late 1800s when showers became what we currently recognize them as. "It was primarily upper-class women who are getting married who would have these showers to assemble a trousseau, which was like the collection of the things that they needed in their married life." They'd get soft things like linens and the like. "And as with most things, and particularly with wedding traditions," Montemurro says, "what started among the elite gradually filtered down to the masses and this became a tradition."

Along that same vein of helping a young bride transition to married life was the custom of building a hope chest. In colonial America, a young woman's family would stock her chest with things that she'd need — soft goods that served to help her transition to married life. Somewhere along the way, things shifted from stocking a chest to hosting an event to help the person getting married.

In some cultures, these events also include an element of cheekiness, to somehow embarrass the bride. Montemurro points to Poland, for example, where a sort of ritualized embarrassment is part of the party. People might place balloons under the bride's chair, one popping every time she takes a seat. In some cultures, this is more sexualized, almost psyching the bride up for the wedding night. This low-grade hazing might be the root of the penis straws common at bachelorette parties today. Women are supposed to prepare to enter married life by amassing things to be a good wife. Men, on the other hand, prepared to enter married life by having a raucous night out. Amazingly, Montemurro points to there being evidence of bachelor parties dating back to ancient Rome.

Bachelorette parties didn't become a thing until the 1960s in North America. Around that time, women started having lingerie showers, which evolved to include alcohol and take place in the evening. The actual term *bachelorette party* wasn't used until the early 1980s, and it grew more popular in the 1990s and early 2000s in Western society. The rise of the bachelorette party happened alongside some sweeping societal changes. Women were becoming increasingly educated, participating more in the labour force. The sentiment was that it's not fair that women have this one boring ritual, the bridal shower, and men get to have this big night out. Women wanted to have the same thing.

Women becoming more independent, economically and socially, set the stage for having a ritual like a bachelorette party to mark the same thing as bachelor parties: the loss of wild, carefree singledom. From blackening the bride in Scotland (essentially kidnapping the bride and/ or groom, getting them filthy, then cleaning them up, pre-wedding day), to dares to get as many kisses from strangers as possible on a hen's night in the U.K., bachelorette parties have symbolized the transition into married life by marking the foolish fun that women are supposed to grow out of.

Gendering of the Pre-Wedding Parties

While the roots of bridal showers harken to a woman's worth (a sweet dowry and a kit of stuff all the better to keep a nice home for her husband), hundreds of years later there is still a bit of a hangover from this. With the average age for marriage getting later (according to the 2017 General Social Survey in Canada, the average age for men to marry is 30 years old, 28 for women), we likely aren't setting up a household from scratch. Couples, for the most part, already have their own stuff from either living alone or shacking up before marriage. Practically speaking, we need less yet there is huge commercial pressure to get everything new when you get married. Not necessary, and also not great for the environment.

Even if we park the notion of how wasteful this is, what does it say that women have showers to get the gear for the house, with only other women? Where are the dudes in all this? Pre-wedding events, in addition to being exorbitantly expensive (hey, someone had to say it!), are literally organized by gender, which, when you think about it, is pretty messed up. Women can only celebrate with their women friends? Men can only celebrate with other men?

Moreover, there's no male equivalent to the bridal shower. Montemurro attests to that in her research. "All the women that I interviewed had bridal showers. Many had bachelorette parties, but not everybody had both. And if they didn't have one, the one that they *didn't have* was the bachelorette party."

Showers perpetuate that women care about pots and pans more than men because this is our area of expertise. What about all the other practical stuff that both halves of a couple need? An iron, lawn mower, BBQ, and whatever else doesn't fall tidily into the bridal category? Are we making protest signs right now advocating "DOWN WITH SHOWERS"? No. But we're advocating that all wedding preparations are less gendered. If you're building the household as a couple, then both parties should be part of making all that happen.

Rethinking Stags and Stagettes

It's safe to say that men aren't coming together to prepare each other for domestic life. When men celebrate their final single days before tying the knot, it might be explicitly around one last night of sexual freedom. Yet for women celebrating a bachelorette, it is more about the ridiculousness and embarrassment. Is a bride actually supposed to be turned on by a male stripper air-humping near her face? Not one bit. It's supposed to be mortifying.

One recent groom, SF, thinks the bachelor party at a strip club is not just passé, but contemptible.[99] "My (former) brother-in-law threw me a bachelor party, but I really wasn't that into it. The whole idea of hanging out in a strip club wasn't part of my scene," he explained. "For the first part of the night we went to the racetrack, watched some horse races. Then when it was time to go to a strip club, I made sure we went to the dive one, the one that reeks of male failure. I remember being like 19 and thinking strip clubs are exciting, now they are boring and depressing. I don't get it. I think there is a misogynistic link between bachelor parties and strip clubs that comes from a really narrow idea of what a marriage is. This sense that you're locked down, all your parties are over forever. Well, you're locked in now. Party's over."

Lewis, a Toronto man, has little joy for the bachelor party as it is currently most celebrated. "I find bachelor parties exhausting. I realize that there are men out there for whom a weekend spent drinking and overeating and hanging out exclusively with other men with no alone time and very little sleep is a dream come true. I'm not sure what to call these men. Extroverts? Troopers? Men's men? Alcoholics? Regardless, I'm not one of them. It takes me a long time to recover after a bachelor party, and it takes my bank account even longer."

He also points to what's more concerning than a jacked-up credit card bill, heartburn, and a colossal hangover. "I'm also a bit dismayed by the gender dynamics that emerge during the lead-up to a wedding. I have a mixed-gender group of friends: men hang out with women; women hang out with men. We don't separate ourselves along gender lines — that is, until somebody gets married, and suddenly we're doing gender-exclusive bachelor parties and gender-exclusive wedding parties. It's a reversion to norms I thought we'd rejected. And it's depressing."

In a way, back in the day, bachelorette parties were sort of progressive, because they societally acknowledged that women also give up their singledom when they marry. The party was over for them, too. But what are we really lauding here, the end of singledom, or the start of a marriage? Co-ed parties are becoming more common, which is a recognition that men are also vested in setting up a home for married life and that men and women and non-binary people can have platonic relationships with someone of another sex. They can, and should, also be super stoked about starting married life. That's not exclusively women's business.

So what does this mean? If you're feeling like a shower is definitely your thing, what about a co-ed one? As a generation, we need to get honest with ourselves about why we take pains to create equitable marriages and then participate in events that literally reinforce gender binaries. One more time for the people in the back: Start your marriage as you mean to continue it.

ASSEMBLING YOUR WEDDING DREAM TEAM

Raise your hand if, like us, you cringe and think, "Oh, wow, those poor people" when you see a wedding party that has like 10 to 15 people per side? Don't get us wrong, if you have that many people who want to stand up for you, you are doing something right. But wrangling that many

Acknowledging the Awkwardness that Is Ranking Your Friends

When you think about it, isn't it a little messed up that we essentially rank our friends for our wedding parties? Back to junior high, picking our best friend, second-best friend, and so on. If it's an easy, no-brainer choice for you to pick your wedding party, do it. If it isn't and you're stressing out about ranking your friends, then don't do it. You each get one representative to sign your marriage licence as a witness, and voilà. Done.

people (and all those personalities) for fittings, pictures, speeches, and meals, requires someone dedicated to spreadsheets and contact lists for, well, months prior to, leading up to, and on the actual wedding date. The irony is that of the countless couples we spoke to while writing this book, regardless of where they lived in the world, their cultural or religious backgrounds, almost all of them shared this sentiment: For a day that is supposed to be all about us, we sure spent a lot of time doing things to placate other people.

There are no rules when it comes to choosing your wedding party, though it makes sense that its scale fits your wedding — a grand wedding party of a dozen attendants on either side might seem out of place at a casual, intimate wedding venue, for example. Beyond the two witnesses who will sign your registry (traditionally the maid of honour and best man), your wedding party can take whatever shape you'd like it to.

As for concerns about having an equal number of bridesmaids and groomsmen, it is a notion that serves to produce a good deal of stress and little else, it seems. If your best friend is a man, then who is better suited to be your right hand? If you are extremely close to two friends and your partner is one of four brothers, then have at it — a perfect posse! The point is not to produce perfect photos. Do a gut check: The crux is to mark a major milestone with those you can't imagine not sharing it with. It doesn't matter if your wedding party is symmetrical, or of the same-sex.

Since when are men and women not friends? The gender constructs of weddings bleed into all sorts of areas, including bridal parties. As if every couple getting married just happens to have a perfectly even number of best men and women friends. Who cares about having symmetrical wedding photos? Focus more on having a ball with the people you love the most. Have a best woman, a man of honour, a mashup of your nearest and dearest, or toss the whole wedding party altogether.

Whether you choose to have one attendant or six, the decision of who will be your supporting cast for the big day is a great one. Your wedding party will not only play a key role in the activities leading up to the wedding (and, of course, behind the scenes at the wedding), their presence is also very sentimental. These are the people who you and your partner have chosen to have closest to you on the day you officially start your life together. Heavy stuff, right?

Having Uncomfortable Conversations

Guilt, fear of hurt feelings, and a sense of obligation can often creep into decisions when selecting your wedding party, so be mindful to really take emotional inventory. If you were a bridesmaid in a friend's wedding, that does not mean that you are obligated to ask them to stand in yours. If there are no small children in your family whom you are close with, do not feel compelled to wrangle two toddlers to serve as a flower girl or ring bearer, just for the sake of having them. The decisions you make should be sincere and heartfelt, rather than couched in obligations.

Whether you want an extended wedding party or none at all (we both went without, so maybe we're a bit biased here), you can have it however you would like, without causing any major friction between you, your friends, and your family. And, we can't stress this enough, like most of the advice in this book, it's all about communication, baby.

It's worth noting, in a big way, that as long as your communication is open — you explain your side of things in a timely, thoughtful, and frank manner — you can't control how others will react. Your friend from college may be hurt that they weren't asked to be in the wedding party, and your sister/brother might not like it if you decide not to have a wedding party at all! Do your best to be polite and gracious in your explanation but know that you can't please everyone. If the other person has your best interests at heart, even if they bristled in the beginning, they're likely to come around. And if they don't, remain calm, and be the bigger person. Stand your ground but be sympathetic to where they're coming from. You don't have to change something because they want you to but coming from a place of understanding may help. Simply saying, "I hear you, and I am sorry that you are hurt, that wasn't our intention, we're doing this because of XYZ/we wanted to!" You will likely be able to assuage some hurt feelings with a little calm and understanding.

If they don't meet you where you are, you are also allowed a cooling-off period. Meaning, you should cool off before you delete them from your invite list entirely. Hasty decisions made around such emotional events may come back to haunt and hurt you later. We suggest taking a week or two, if you're far out from the actual date.

Sometimes things don't go according to plan and someone might back out of your wedding party a few months before the big day. Don't take it personally. (Unless they backed out because your wedding has turned you into a monster, in which case, take that to heart, big time.) Sometimes people can't make the time, travel, or expenses of being in a wedding party work. Whichever way people have supported you, thank them sincerely and in writing.

Be careful if you are considering filling their spot. It might have a stink of "second choice" about it for the person you ask, particularly if they know you picked someone ahead of them.

When we really get down to the essentials (which we should be pretty well versed in in this post-pandemic world), enjoying the moment is key. And having the people who bring you joy closest to you at your wedding will help assuage any ickiness that may arise. As psychology dictates, friends are people we surround ourselves with voluntarily, where we have a mutual respect for each other, there is a sense of reciprocity, and, above all else, you take pleasure in spending time with. Lean on this core group of pals when something sly comes from a distant relative or all your vases break the day of the wedding. Your people will be more than happy to change the conversation or run out for replacement vases at a moment's notice. Like you would do for them in a "big day" pinch.

Be sure to give people at least six months' notice and help them where you can. They will be paying for their own travel and wedding attire, so if you can help with anything else (like a place to stay, for example), it is really nice to offer it up.

Assigning Your Dream Team Tasks

Your best person and/or person of honour can expect to be responsible for the following:

- Plays the role of the couple's air traffic controller, helping to ensure everyone knows what to wear, where to show up, and at what time.
- Typically helps write down who gave what at showers or parties, so thank-you notes can be swiftly sent.
- Helpfully communicates registry information.
- Assists with the seating chart.
- Helps the bride or groom shop for an outfit and other wearables for the wedding. If that's their thing.
- Hosts (or co-hosts) a shower or party for the couple.
- On the wedding day helps the couple with their sartorial needs. (Can you fasten a bustle? Tie a bow tie? GO LEARN.)
- Holds one of the two rings before the ceremony and if a bouquet is being carried, this person holds it during the vows.
- Signs the registry.
- Stands in the receiving line.
- Graciously gives a thoughtful toast to the couple.
- Helps on the wedding day to assist with vendors.
- Helps to safely store gifts and, later, if they are really nice, drop them off at your home.

Understanding Your Wedding Party's Responsibilities

Wedding party duties may vary, but here are some jobs that can help make everyone's day a run a little smoother:

- Lavishes the special couple with love, attention, and warm wishes — their chief responsibility.
- Listens sympathetically and tops up glasses while the couple need to vent.
- Attends wedding-related activities including the shower, the rehearsal, the wedding (of course), and post-wedding festivities like a next-day brunch or lunch.
- Pays for their attire, with the exception of flowers. The cost of bouquets and boutonnieres are not the responsibility of the wedding party.
- If pre-wedding primping is arranged, each attendant pays for their own hair, makeup, nails, and such. (You can talk about a look you're going for, but you don't get to dictate how anyone's hair is styled or makeup is done.)
- Arranges and foots the bill for their own transportation, though it is a nice gesture for the couple to host them if they are from out of town.
- Stands in the receiving line.
- Is generally helpful at the wedding, directing people to the guest-book, bar, gifts table, and so on.

Asking for Help (You Can Do It!)

No one, and we mean no one, will care about your wedding as much as you do. Many people will ask how your planning is going purely out of politeness or for an opportunity to reminisce about their wedding. You walk a fine balance between wanting people to feel included but not feeling like an imposition. You don't want to isolate anyone, nor do you want to lean on anyone too hard. But, may we suggest, when people offer to help, be open to it.

We unabashedly advocate for minimal wedding stress, but even the most organized couple still has a lot of things to consider and, well, do. These are some tasks that are perfect to enlist others to take on:

Confirming your vendors. A few weeks before your wedding, it is a great idea to call up everyone to make sure they've got things in order. You can just as easily pass this list to someone else to make some calls, confirm rates, times, and all those annoying-but-super-important details.

Getting people paid. If you have vendors that need to be paid, give your envelopes of cash to someone else to hand over.

Hot Tip: Don't Be a Taskmaster

Maybe you've read about or been a part of bridal parties that have weekly conference calls or "team meetings." Sorry, just no. Asking someone to be part of your wedding is taxing enough. Asking them to carve out regular time for it is indulgent and you run the risk of annoying people. That said, get yourself organized and be communicative. Just don't be a taskmaster about it.

Next-day nibbles. If you are having lots of overnight guests or out-of-towners, someone could totally make some coffee and put out some pastries for a quick get-together before everyone hits the road. We beseech you: Do not do this yourself. You'll be exhausted the morning after the wedding (and hopefully not just from dancing, WINK WINK).

Decor. If you're making your own centrepieces, bouquets, or decorating an area, get others to help. Get twice the number of people you think you need and allocate a full hour more than you expect it will take.

Helping your photographer. You might want to do up a quick shot list if there are photos that you know you'll want (special out-of-town guests, for example, or your grandparents). Pair your photographer up with someone who knows all of these key people, so they don't need to flag you down to ask who is who.

Gifts at the reception. If you are receiving gifts, make sure someone in your wedding party can direct people where to place those gifts or make sure the table is in an area where people can spot it.

Packing up at the end of the night. If you have decorations or anything that has to leave the venue that night, ask a trusted someone to please bring these items with them.

Your go-to person. If you know there are things that are going to chap your ass that day, write a list of them and give them to someone who can handle it. It could be bad music, people doing shots, the washrooms getting messy, those sorts of things. Write them on a list and ask a confidante to stay on top of them.

Looking for Your Master of Ceremonies

By no means necessary, if you'd like to have a master of ceremonies, this is suited to a person who is one-part host to one-part project manager. Charismatic and comfortable speaking to a crowd, they will be tasked with keeping your toasts on track and sharing some anecdotes about you as a couple.

Your emcee should also be

- someone who isn't shy and can project their voice well;
- someone who can give structure and direction during the event, otherwise things may feel unorganized to the guests;
- someone to welcome the newly wedded couple into the reception; and
- someone who can give instructions to guests arriving at the reception so that people in the wedding party don't have to do this, especially if they're away from the reception for pictures, receiving lines, etc.

If there's no emcee, make sure you've planned the speaking order, that those speaking know what the order is and that they know when to start (and end!) their remarks.

PLANNING DOS AND DON'TS FOR YOUR RECEPTION

Most people have fun at weddings (unless the wedding sucks, of course), but there are some absolute buzzkills that you should pay attention to, in our humble opinion.

Working with the Venue

Accessibility. Can people get into the space, move around, and use the washroom? Think about your guests who aren't as mobile or able-bodied. Guests of a certain age might have a hard time with stairs, too.

Number of washrooms. Seriously. There is nothing worse than no place to pee. Don't have a one stall for 100 people type situation. Just don't.

Condition of washrooms. Second only to a lack of place to pee is a place to pee that is disgusting. Ask your venue if someone, anyone, can do a mid-wedding check-in to empty the garbage, restock toilet paper, or wipe down the toilets. Or ask a friend who really, really, really loves you.

Rain plan. If your wedding is at all exposed to the elements, plan for the worst so your guests stay comfortable. A freezing room that feels like an icebox, squeezing like sardines under one giant golf umbrella in a downpour, or a sauna-like space where you're sweating without even moving, are sure ways for people to remember what a miserable time they had at your wedding.

Elbow room. Does it feel like the subway during rush hour? Just because your venue can accommodate a certain number of people in their fire code doesn't mean that you need exactly that many people there. And given that we may be social distancing well into the 2020s, the more space you allow the better. On that, have you heard that couples should plan for 10 percent of those invited not to come? Yeah, no. That is a made-up statistic. If you are inviting 150 people, plan on 150 to be in attendance.

Thinking Ahead to Your Guest Experience

Yes, you want to have a languorous, lovely wedding day, but sometimes less is more. People never, ever complain about weddings that err on the short-and-sweet side. A long ceremony followed by a long cocktail hour followed by a long dinner followed by long speeches will have your guests longing to get the heck out of there.

Hot Tip: Take Photos Before the Ceremony

Many couples have their ceremony, then take off with their new spouse and possibly family and wedding party for a few hours to go take photos, which is, like, fine. Except for your wedding guests, who get bored and start trash talking you. Your wedding guests are there to see you, after all, so don't take off for three hours. Why not have an intimate little moment before the wedding, where you and your honey spend some time together, snap some pics, ask your nearest and dearest to join you, snap some more pics, then go immediately from wedding to reception/ party mode. It is so much more efficient for everyone, including your guests, and often easier on your budget.

If you are asking people to arrive at a time when they are typically fed, don't leave them starving through a two-hour ceremony or a number of speeches. "This doesn't mean you need an elaborate meal that stuffs people to the gills," says event planner Allison Slight. "It just takes some planning, and some know-how."

When planning your music, she recommends not over-catering to one single group. If you play only music that under-30-year-olds will like, the dance floor will be a slow start. Consider the older crowd who will dance first and leave early. "And don't have an expectation that everyone will dance. It might not happen," she warns.

If you are looking at splurging on linens, glassware, cutlery, and so on, if you have a really specific design in mind, go for it, but only some people will notice and these accoutrements add up quickly, Slight says.

Special stations and installations that are great for guests' Instagram are popping up more and more. If you

ENSURE ALL OF YOUR GUESTS
EQUALLY ENJOY THEMSELVES

Rebecca Anger, a Chicago-based disabled social activist, says a little thoughtfulness goes a long way. Not every disability is visible, so take care to try to create an experience that all of your guests can equally enjoy. For example, if your venue is accessible but only by a side or back entrance (as was the case where Rebecca got married herself), set it up so all of your guests use that same entrance. "When all your guests use the same entrance, no one feels othered," says Anger. She also mentions sight lines, an easy thing to overlook. "I've been to weddings where I couldn't see at all, as I use a wheelchair. We arranged our room for our ceremony to give people using wheelchairs or other devices the best views and asked everyone to stay seated." She also recommends ensuring that your room can be easily manoeuvred by people using devices, and that single-stall washrooms are easier to navigate (and, let's be honest, gendered washrooms are problematic for a lot of reasons, anyway). Make sure you have ample seating throughout, and, if you can swing it, it is a nice idea to create a quiet room with low sensory experience. "Spaces like this are great for anyone to go and decompress, but particularly for people with fatigue, chronic pain, or those who are on the spectrum," says Anger.*

---

* Rebecca Anger, in discussion with Karen Cleveland, September 6, 2020.

have extra money after all of your priorities are covered, great, but don't build your wedding around having a photo booth, for example, she cautions. Likewise with anything else precious like an elaborate sweet table. Those things are all extra, so do them last.

Assembling Your Seating Plans

If you are planning a seated dinner of any size, organize your seating so your guests aren't wondering where the heck they are seated.

Since we're on the subject of seating, we're all for saying goodbye to the ceremony seating that divides the two families of the couple. The whole point is two families coming together anyway, right?

Or you can say hard pass, host your reception cocktail-party style, and skip the grief of a seating arrangement all together. Seriously, it is a great option.

If you're set on a seated dinner, think less about dividing the room in half for your families and think more about some strategic cross-pollination. Put your most fun friends at the table mixed with your outgoing cousins who don't know anyone their age. Think about building tables around common interests or social circles, or even generations. Your great-aunts on either side of the family might enjoy sitting with like-minded ladies. Don't have a token singles table as a catch all for anyone else that doesn't fit tidily into your tables. Seat them with friends, even if it means squeezing 11 people around a 10-person table.

Organizing the Wedding Toasts

Since when did toasting the happy couple turn into 10-minute speeches? Wedding toasts can be dreadful. We have all sat through cringe-worthy ramblings during a reception. Perhaps the speaker helped themselves to a bit too much liquid courage, blabbed on for ages, or made unfortunate digs at the couple that went beyond good-natured jokes. No one likes to be humiliated, particularly in public and certainly not at their wedding.

A great speaker can woo a room into a chuckle, or a tear, and every couple wants to feel good, warm fuzzy vibes from anyone speaking at their wedding. Here are five essential tips to make sure your wedding toasts are delivered without a hitch:

- Decide exactly who you want to give toasts and encourage them to please be brief. Three to five minutes is a long window of time to fill. By encouraging your speakers to keep their wedding speeches short and sweet, you might also ease any pressure that they have put on themselves to go on at length. If you say three minutes at the absolute max, they might go on for five, tops. Let's hope.
- Choose speakers that you feel confident can handle the task gracefully. If you have concerns about your maid of honour being too nervous or too lengthy, perhaps you could pair her up with the best man? Strength in numbers!
- If there is a particular speaker that you worry might go rogue, or tell that one humiliating story, speak to them privately and share your concern. Look them dead in the eye and confide that you will undoubtedly be emotional on your wedding day and could use their support in holding it together, particularly during toasts. Hopefully, as a good friend, they'll concede and take it easy on you. Request that your emcee or another pal keep things running smoothly on your behalf.
- Relax. Once you have set the stage, so to speak, it is out of your hands. Sit back and revel in the love.

Making Those Introductions

At your ceremony, have your officiant introduce people.

At your reception, have your emcee or someone introduce who is speaking. It takes a ton of pressure off the speaker, wondering when they are supposed to get up to speak. An introduction also helps provide a bit of context so your other guests know who this person speaking is ("And now, Tom, the groom's friend, will read the couple's favourite poem").

• •

Real-Life Wedding Stories

SF realized that a wedding does not make the marriage.

"We got married on the beach in the Dominican Republic with about 30 guests. I had nothing to do with the planning, I was in Sudan. We had agreed on the location and that was it.

"I got back from my tour in April and we got married in May, and I didn't even stick around for those weeks in between. I went to New Orleans. I was really stressed. I didn't want to go through with getting married at that time. I felt it was too soon. I was feeling too unsettled. We were in a rough stretch in our relationship with me being deployed for six months, it almost ended our relationship, then I got back from tour and the wedding was weeks away.

"In hindsight, I think [for my wife] immersing herself in planning the wedding was a way to feel close to me while I was away. It took us a few years to get it together. I had to get my own stuff together. We're now flourishing as a couple. Our experience is that the marriage, not the wedding, matters.

"One thing that was important to both of us was our first dance. My wife is a dancer, so we choreographed it together — our first dance and the parents' dance. It was important to me to participate in that. I picked some movements that I thought were nice and she made them look better. We rehearsed, did a lot of practising in the kitchen, we even borrowed a studio space. Right before the wedding we ran through it with our parents. Looking back, it was the most intimate part of the night, performing something we created together. Whenever we go to weddings now, it is this big point of pride that our first dance was better."

* * *

Paulina and Sandy got hitched in a pinch.

Sandy and Paulina met at a gay bar in Guadalajara, Jalisco, Mexico. Neither were looking for a serious relationship: Paulina hadn't yet come out to her family and Sandy had recently broken up with a serious long-time partner. But cupid didn't care. They exchanged numbers and started dating. A year later they started living together and moved to Vancouver, where Paulina has family. After living there for one year, they were both on the same page about staying in Canada.

For a few years they had talked about what a wedding could look like. Then, Covid-19 arrived and, coupled with making plans to stay in Canada, things started moving quickly. "We realized that our best next step should be to get married in Canada," explained Paulina. They were both utterly devoted to each other, had a shared future mapped out, and knew they were a great team. They had precisely one month before they had to fly back to Mexico, so they organized everything in two weeks. They wanted something simple and private, with a bit of a vintage feel.

The momentum tested their resolve. "At the beginning we started to forget about the simple and private thing because we were so excited about it. We wanted everyone to have an unforgettable and pleasant time, but we were actually forgetting about ourselves, and we were acting like a 'traditional couple getting married.' In Mexico we call that behaviour 'to throw the house out of the window' and this means that you want to make a huge and unforgettable party that implies spending a lot of money (on probably unnecessary things). I think in English it's 'to spare no expense,'" said Paulina. They wanted family to fly in from Mexico but between the short timelines and the pandemic, it just wasn't a possibility.

"We just decided to do it our way and whoever wanted to come was invited," said Paulina. Family from the Vancouver area made the trip, along with a small group of friends, for a total of 13 guests, with more joining by video conference. Unfortunately, some family from Mexico were less than supportive, but it didn't dampen the mood. The couple like the beach and the woods, but the officiant that they liked could only do it in North Vancouver. They landed on a gazebo in North Vancouver, with a honeymoon in Whistler (a wedding gift from Paulina's dad).

"We did feel that heteronormative pressure of weddings. We wanted to buy wedding suits instead of wedding dresses and realized there were no easy options. When buying decorations for our wedding cake, everything was 'Mr. and Mrs.' We just did us. We wore the same coloured suits, wore heels and veils, and carried bouquets," said Paulina.

Friends pitched in to do hair and makeup and take photos. After the ceremony, they went to a local restaurant for dinner. They ordered two cakes from their favourite bakery and asked to write Ms. & Ms. on each of them. The night was capped off by the couple dancing to their song, "The Way You Look Tonight," before racing off for a romantic weekend in Whistler. "We both enjoyed it so much, I think because we didn't have much expectations, or even the chance to create them" said Paulina. "We are just so grateful. We were surrounded by love and good vibes, that's all we ever wanted."

10 The Day and Every Day After

We Want You to Enjoy Your Wedding and Your Marriage

You're getting married today! YEEEEAH! It's going to be a straight-up blast. You've been true to yourself throughout the planning process. You and your beloved are psyched to marry each other and celebrate your love in front of the people who matter the most to you. You've got a licence to wed, hot outfits, a photographer to capture the magic, and enough food and drink for everyone to be merry. You're set, right?

GETTING YOU PROPERLY, AND HAPPILY, HITCHED

Start the Day Right

Get some rest the night before your wedding. Honestly. It's hard having guests in from out of town and not wanting to stay out all night with them catching up, but get thee to bed. You want to wake up refreshed, which likely means a solid night's sleep, with no hangover. Have a coffee with your honey and get all stoked together. Eat a good breakfast, too.

Pack the Night Before

Don't leave packing until last minute. Bring your ring, your marriage licence, and things you'll need at the reception or the next morning (like medication and/or birth control).

Do Your Nails Days Before

To you riverboat gamblers considering booking manicures for their wedding day, a word of caution. That takes HOURS to dry and you don't have hours to do nothing, we expect. If getting your nails done is your thing, do it the day before or get one of those long-lasting gel manicures that don't render your hands useless for hours.

Primp to Look Your Best

Some advice? Don't try a new product or treatment that day (lest you have a reaction and your skin freaks out) or change your appearance drastically (not the day to get a haircut, change hair colour, try fake nails, or get your brows tinted, trust).

If you are getting dolled up, wear a shirt that buttons up, so you don't mess up your hair and makeup by pulling a T-shirt over your head. (This sounds like such basic, basic advice and yet …)

YOU NEED A WEDDING DAY KIT

You likely won't have your giant purse to schlep all your stuff, so having a little stash of necessities is a good idea. You can leave it someplace at the venue or give it to a friend. Pop in Tylenol, floss, some mints, CBD balm to help with any foot pain, a mini first-aid kit, mini deodorant, blotting papers, tampons, and a stain-remover pen. Also: toss some moleskin in there too. That stuff is MAGIC for pinchy shoes, and blisters are a sure-fire way to put a damper on your wedding.

Get Ready Your Way

There's no right way or traditional way to get ready for your wedding. Maybe you're a private person and really want to find time to be introspective and alone on your wedding day. Some people might want the party vibe to start early and are big into the "getting ready with the gang" situation. You might want to help your mom get her makeup just right, or that idea might stress you out. Do whatever feels good, because those hours before the hoopla starts are pretty precious.

Eat something, maybe go for a run, or a squeeze in some yoga if that's your thing.

I, Karen, personally enjoy getting ready alone (sometimes with a glass of something bubbly or coffee in hand), with the music up. On my wedding day, my guy and I got ready together (there was champagne, there was cheese, and, I think, James Brown). It was a blast. If you are not returning to the space where you get ready, plan for someone to grab your stuff or store it. Plan for travel time, too, of course.

Asking for (and Accepting) Help on the Actual Wedding Day

Some people are really, really good at asking for help, the rest of us are not. Particularly because we're talking a big game in this book about keeping things low-key, you still don't want to be running around on your wedding day. Not because you can't, but because you should be having fun. So, you won't want the caterer asking you to confirm the number of vegan meals the morning of the wedding. You don't want the DJ asking if there is an extension cord she can borrow. You don't want to be dealing with any of that. Not on your wedding day.

Pre-Wedding Gift Exchange

A few couples we spoke to have some very strong feelings about wedding-day gifts.

"Apparently pre-wedding gifts are a thing, where she's in her silk robe reading a letter that he wrote her saying how he can't wait to marry her that day while opening up a diamond tennis bracelet from him or something like that. It is an unabashed flaunting of wealth. It also creates this other pressure, as if there isn't enough pressure tied to weddings, like 'What did YOUR husband get you on your wedding day?' Uhhh, duh, a wedding. We got each other a wedding."

If you can enlist the help of a friend (that friend we keep talking about this whole book, the one who is super organized and helpful and on top of stuff), ask if they'll be your point person. Give them the plan for the day, ensure your vendors have their contact information, and they have your vendors' contact information and copies of contracts/agreements. Then sit back and let them do what you asked them to do: They can sort out any final details, troubleshoot on your behalf, and settle up if you give them means of payment.

Asking for help might also include things like asking a friend to do your hair, put some flowers together, grab a few bags of ice, feed your cat. You get where we're going. Life is busy. Life on your wedding day is a special kind of busy.

Here's the thing though: You are asking your friends for help, not paying them for their services. So, if you are super particular about how your hair looks or how those flowers get arranged, either chill and let your friend do their best, or pay someone to make it exactly how you want it. We're of the "chill and say thank you" mind, but you do you.

Checking In with Your Venue and Vendors

You might want to plan a check in with the venue a few hours ahead, even if it's a text to be like, "Hey, all good over there?" Just to help you get in front of anything that needs troubleshooting, you know? Whether you have a wedding coordinator, a trusted friend who is good with the details, or just want to check in yourself, it is a good idea to quickly touch base. Know who is your point person for anything that might go wrong, so you can play air traffic controller to get the right people to figure stuff out. Regardless of how small or low-key your wedding is, you definitely want everyone's name and phone number at your fingertips. Copies of any contracts or agreements don't hurt, either.

Here's our cheat sheet of whose contact information to have on hand:

- officiant
- photographer
- florist
- venue contact (if anyone is catering, delivering food or booze, or anything else)
- both sets of parents or key people
- DJ/band/person playing their Spotify playlist for you
- your contact for transportation

Paying People the Day Of

You might actually need to pay some people on your wedding day, so do a quick run through of who you need to pay and when, bring along a credit card or cheque(s), and pass them along to your point person if you have one.

On the topic of money, you might get cash among your gifts at the wedding. Ask someone to collect it for you at the end of the night. Don't even think of bringing it on your honeymoon if you are leaving straight away.

HAVING A VERY, VERY GOOD WEDDING DAY

Take in the Ceremony

There's this really amazing moment, just as you are ready to say your vows, when you can literally feel the love in the room. Be in the moment as you stare into your beloved's eyes, but take a minute to look at your guests, too. Seriously. Turn back and face your guests for just a moment and marvel in the people that have come to your wedding because they love you, want to celebrate you, and are rooting for your marriage.

Consider Drinking Less

Technically, you're not supposed to be drinking to yourselves during all those lovely toasts, but you can bet that once the champagne starts flowing, it is easy to get carried away. It is your prerogative if you want to get silly, but if you want to be totally present and remember every detail, consider some non-alcoholic drinks for you and your new spouse. Ask the bar or caterer to pour from a bottle of non-alcoholic champagne or wine or mix mocktails. Even if you do this for half the night, you'll be more clearheaded for the night. You can keep it your little secret, too.

Find Time for Each Other

You're going to feel so incredibly popular, trying to say hello to everyone while soaking up all the warm, fuzzy congratulations. It is THE BEST! Quite likely, you and your partner might get separated throughout the night (or morning, or afternoon, you know what we mean). Try to make a point to keep an eye on the clock to meet on the half hour, for example. Set an alarm on your phone if needed. And find time to steal away for a few little make-out sessions, too. You will not regret this.

Make Time to Eat

The day of your wedding is going to fly by! So much so that you might forget to eat. Drink a glass of water on the hour (you could even ask a buddy to remind you) and if you can't find time to sit down for your entire meal, ask your caterer to set aside a plate of something for you and your love to eat. Some will even make a little to-go package so you can snack after the wedding.

Make Time for Your Folks

Your wedding day is a big deal for your parents or those who fulfill that role in your life. Whether they co-planned it, you butted heads a bit, or whatever, make a point to find them and tell them how much you love them. We bet they'd like some pictures together or a little turn on the dance floor, too.

Stay Somewhere Amazing on Your Wedding Night

Maybe you're practical and are thinking, "Nah, we'll just cab home that night and stay in our apartment" or "Oh! Aunt-so-and-so is nearby, let's just stay with family and save more money toward the honeymoon." Nope. No way.

Book a hotel room or room at an inn. Splurge on staying some-place great. Have your shit sent to the hotel the day before so there is one less thing to think about on your wedding day. When you're booking, it doesn't hurt to mention that it is your wedding night. You might get an upgrade or a nice treat in your room. While we're on the subject of your wedding night, you might have transformative mind-blowing sex, or you might pass out from the exhaustion from your wedding. Whatever happens is yours and it's great, so just roll with it, with no expectations.

GATHERING TIPS FROM RECENTLY MARRIED COUPLES

What did we miss? Everyone's got their best tip, so we rounded up some from recently married couples.*

- Go with the flow! Things will, without question, not go exactly as you planned. Roll with it.
- Ask people to be in charge of the big things. Everyone took their jobs seriously and tried not to bother me with dumb questions.
- I made a Google Doc of who/where/when for all our vendors with delivery times. I also put money into envelopes for all my outstanding payments.
- Plan for clean up! I was left with a bunch of drunkies and no one to help clean up the venue at the end of the night. Whoops.
- Plan on doing absolutely NOTHING on the wedding day, if you can. I made lists upon lists and delegated everything I could think of, from who is setting out the guestbook to who is picking up our morning bagel order (with cash I'd set aside the week before to give them). And it was so worth it. I honestly didn't know if I could let go and be present in the day, but because finally, after months, there was nothing left to actually do, I was able to just let it be.

---

* Shout-out to our friends and Reddit.

- Be a guest at your own wedding. Enjoy all the great things that you wanted and planned for. Don't criticize them or look to see if they measure up, just have a really great time.
- Plan breaks, and during those breaks have someone you trust check in with you to see if there is anything they can take off your plate (or your mind).
- Be kind to yourself in the days leading up to your wedding so that you have as many emotional resources as possible. Don't underestimate how emotionally depleting it is.

WELCOMING YOURSELF TO MARRIED LIFE! THE WEEKS RIGHT AFTER YOUR WEDDING

Even if you aren't hosting a full-on day after the wedding, it is nice to keep the party going in a low-key way. That might mean getting coffee or brunch with people who came in from out of town.

You might also want to both sit down a day or two after the wedding and write down your best moments from the day. When it is fresh, we all say to ourselves, "I will never forget a moment of this" and guess what? We all do. Write it down so you can revisit your wedding day whenever you want.

Getting Those Thank-You Cards Out

If there is one holdover from the fusty old way of getting married, to us, it is thank-you notes. We're big fans. Not only does it show your appreciation for someone (gratitude is a wonderful, mood-boosting thing!), but it also adds a nice sense of closure to all your wedding festivities (see page 32 for tips).

Yeah, yeah there are official rules about how long people have to send a gift and how long you get until you need to say thank you for said gift, but just trust us and do it early. Divide it up between you, get two pens, two stacks of cards (no digital thank yous, go old school here), and just write thank yous like it's your job. Remember our earlier advice about setting up a document to track who got you what gift? Now is the time to find it so you can be specific in your thank-you notes.

Here's a strategic way to approach sending out those cards:

- Yes, there is the adage that you should send out your thank-you notes within at least one year after getting married. But try to do it ASAP. It will help stop any procrastinating tendencies off the bat.
- Obviously you should hit up everyone who attended the ceremony and/or party. And some etiquette peeps will mention also thanking the vendors that you worked with. If a vendor truly made your day extra special, have it at. But likely the best way to thank a vendor is by leaving a nice review/endorsement online. Otherwise, you've already paid them with actual dollars so don't feel like you have to spend precious handwriting muscles on a vendor.
- Don't be afraid to get personal. Especially when addressing close friends and family. Here's a chance to thank them for the big stuff, but also highlight the little things (like picking up so-and-so from the airport, running those errands for you, etc.).
- Or not. If there is someone at your wedding you don't feel particularly close with, a thank-you note is still absolutely needed, but simplicity can be key here. If they bought you a gift, definitely mention it, and potentially note how it has added value to your life. But don't feel the need to go too flowery or OTT. It will come off as insincere, at least to you, and will likely make you and potentially the guest feel icky.
- Have new pens, your thank-you cards, stamps, and your gift list at the ready. Sit down one night with your new spouse and get through as many as you can. You can even start by simply addressing the envelopes one night, then getting onto the note writing another. If you need to break things up even further, concentrate on those who travelled from afar to be there on your wedding day first. They made the biggest sacrifice after all.

QUICK, PUT THIS IN YOUR CALENDAR

A week before your first wedding anniversary, tell your partner that you're going to take your rings to get cleaned, so they are sparkling. Get them cleaned, but also sneakily take them to have them engraved. In tiny type, on the inside of the band, get something special inscribed: your wedding date, your pet name for them, your initials, something sweet that will make them swoon. We bet they won't even notice until you point it out to them on your anniversary.

Letting the Good Times Roll

They don't call it the honeymoon phase for nothing, you know.

Before we get too serious, let's have a little fun. How long can you *actually* milk your honeymoon benefits for? We say one year. You're ideally only going to go through this wedded-bliss phase once in your life, so kick back and don't be afraid to slip it into conversations with hotels, restaurants, and more that you JUST. GOT. MARRIED. At the very least you'll get a nice, warm smile and a congratulations, which will help those fuzzy feelings last, and last, and last. And at the most, you'll get some perks.

Dinner reservation? Tell them you are celebrating your wedding. Hotel stay? Tell them you are celebrating your wedding. Casual beer at your local watering hole? Remind them that you just got married. Do this because you can. Do it for a year. Seriously. People love to send over a round of champagne, wish you a heartfelt congratulations, or tell you about their wedding. Soak up all the good vibes and treats and sweetness. You might even get some pearls of wisdom. Stretch this out because once it is gone, it is gone.

I (Karen) have a really sweet memory from our honeymoon (well, every trip for two years after the wedding was decreed a honeymoon, but this was our first trip the week after our wedding). We were at a tiny greasy spoon in Boston having breakfast and were all swoony with "honeymooners" written all over our faces. An elderly couple came by to share that they got married 70 years ago, the same month that we got married. They wished us well and meant it. Like, really meant it. I will never forget that.

Don't get us wrong, we're not advocating that you take advantage of anyone, but hospitality-type businesses often think ahead for these types of situations, so they may have some extra champagne on hand, or they may be able to upgrade your accommodations or even add in a spa service or two. If you're worried about seeming greedy, make sure to spread the love on the OTT customer service by giving the business a proper shout-out on social media or leaving a great review on their website. And tip generously.

And while the one-year mark is usually a good time to call it when subtly hinting for any extras, you can get away with longer but only *if* your actual honeymoon is planned after your first anniversary.

Understanding the Post-Wedding Crash

Some couples can't wait for their wedding to be over and done with, because they find the whole experience completely exhausting. Others find that they feel pretty down when it is all over.

Alice got married last year and was taken aback by how she felt. "There's a part of weddings that no one talks about — it's the post-wedding depression. After the wedding, I was like IT WAS SO GOOD, then I spent two months feeling so blue. There was all of this build up and excitement leading up to the wedding, then it happened and it was so amazing, then it is over and back to regular life. And for most couples it really is regular life because couples are already living together before they get married. I thought it would feel different or something. It didn't. We got high on the wedding and then there's the come down. People should know about this and talk about it. It is completely unnatural how 'all about the bride' everything is, everyone is so generous with their time, their money, their words. Then the minute the wedding is over, it's like who is going to get married now. It is no longer about you. I wasn't prepared for that low."

KNOWING THAT THE FIRST YEAR MAY BE HARD

Michelle here. Before I got married, I remember my mom, my best friend, and a handful of people telling me that the first year of marriage is the hardest. To be honest, I didn't really believe them. My partner and I had been through some shit (my father died about a year after we first started dating and he was living in and renovating a house with his best friend the first two years of our relationship), so I thought we had everything pretty tight. But boy, I was wrong.

I may have scarred one lovely person with this realization. I was out at a work event one evening when a freshly engaged colleague asked me how married life was, and I looked her dead in the eyes and said, "It sucks!" Her face dropped. My partner and I had been fighting pretty intensely the night before, and I was so exhausted that I had no energy to hide my contempt.

When I saw the colour drain from her face, I backpedalled to the old adage that the first year is the toughest. And I began listing all the good things about my partner and our new life together. I was still frustrated, but it actually helped me put things in perspective. Even though I voiced my feelings, thankfully my pal still pulled the trigger and has been happily married for a few years.

So, why is the first year the hardest? "The first year of marriage is when all of the excitement of the relationship begins to be replaced with routine and structure," says Hannah Esmaili, clinical social work/therapist, M.S.W., M.Ed., C.Psych., R.P., of the Counselling 2

Wellness clinic, who Michelle spoke to in March 2020.[100] "Before the actual first year of marriage, there's the dating period, there's the engagement — all the highs of the relationship. Then when we get to the first year of marriage, this is when it becomes about routine, structure, stability, and the norms of the relationship need to be developed."

What is even more interesting according to Esmaili, is that researchers John and Judy Gottman found that most marriages actually break down at rather specific times in their marriage. While the first year is a tough one, they found that couples actually throw in the towel between years 5 and 7 or years 10 and 12. But if you start from a strong foundation, hopefully this bump will be minor or at the very least, something that can be worked through.

Yes, the first 365 can be a bit of a roller coaster. But don't fret, there are a few relationship tactics that can help with first year angst. "There really has to be effective communication and negotiation, because if that isn't happening, that's when couples get into a lot of the patterns of conflict," Esmaili, who specializes in family and couples' therapy, believes. It's worth noting that Esmaili sees clients of all backgrounds — including LGBTQ couples and couples who come from different ethnic or religious backgrounds — and what she's speaking to applies to couples across the board.

Holding On to Those Newlywed Vibes

But how exactly do you keep those good vibes going well into the first year of marriage and beyond? Hopefully you've set the stage by starting to communicate with your new wedded partner. If you have or haven't, there is always time to brush up on this most important aspect of living as a duo. Communication is key (are you sick of hearing us say this yet?), as is honesty and fairness. You are, in fact, one half of a couple and being upfront is important, but so is compromise in likeminded tasks. While we don't believe that anyone should compromise themselves or their morals for their partner, being able to identify common goals as a family (because you're now officially family) will help you to see things from both yours and your partner's perspective.

That all sounds well and good, but how exactly do you *do* that?

Counselling for Two

According to a 2017 study by MidAmerica Nazarene University, millennials (those born between 1981 and 1996) are more likely to seek relationship counselling than boomers or Gen Xers.[101] We have to say, we really like this trend!

However, 55 percent of women surveyed, versus only 46 percent of males, were interested in seeking help through counselling services. It's perhaps not surprising that more women were down to get real in a therapy room, but with the number of men interested in seeking help as well, we find it very encouraging.

And what is the most common complaint in the couples' therapy room shouldn't surprise you. It's all about communication (that word again!), and connection, says Esmaili. "Did you know you need two-and-a-half hours of talk time a week to maintain a friendship?" And those precious minutes mean "no TV, no gadgets, no disagreements on the table."

Not only will talk time help you bond with your beloved, but connection can be a major area that needs improvement post tying the knot. "What often happens is during the wedding planning and organization, couples often get preoccupied with the details, and the connection between them begins to fizzle," she says. Hence why time together, with no distractions, can really help boost that l-o-v-e quotient.

Esmaili also refers to a couples' counselling term when talking about the first year of marriage. Beware of the Four Horsemen, aka the inability to fight fairly, contempt, criticism and stonewalling. As she explains, "Defensiveness is often this place [where one or both people in] the couple will not take responsibility for whatever's happened [in an argument]. Contempt is this animosity, an environment of hostility that couples will use in disagreements. Criticism is often the attack of the other, rather than speaking to your needs in a positive way. And stonewalling, we know actually happens with all males and females with a history of trauma, [where] they shut down and it's really hard for them to [communicate]."

And last, but certainly not least, Esmaili again points to the research of John and Judy Gottman. The Gottman's have spent 40 years researching couples, and they've created seven tiers of the relationship house, which most couples' counsellors will use to assess any new clients. If you're seeking a counsellor, definitely ask about this approach, which includes ideas such as building a love map (a series of questions that help you remember important things about your beau), sharing fondness and admiration for each other (pretty straightforward!), turning toward your partner instead of away (i.e., stating your needs out loud instead of shutting someone out), and commitment (knowing and believing that this person is your lifelong partner).

Putting Money Matters First

Sadly, those finance rumours are true. According to Esmaili, "We know when couples disagree over finances weekly, the likelihood of them experiencing divorce goes up tremendously." So it will definitely bode well for your new coupledom if you get your finances, and any issues you have around money, in order. Perhaps getting married and working together on all the details should be used as a warm-up to the big money talks that are bound to happen post nuptials?

Considering Family Dynamics

One other bone of contention to watch out for, according to Esmaili, are issues with either side of the family — tension here can tear even the strongest of couples apart. We're not advocating for being a doormat, but learning to deal with difficult in-laws, whatever that looks like for you, can help maintain a status quo in your relationship. If this is a touchy subject for you and your partner, a counsellor can certainly help to get things back on track.

Therapist Steven Giles knows that extended families can be a major source of strife for couples. He explains that in a marriage, each person is entering into their partner's family of origin. "The tendency is, I know how to operate very well in my family and my partner has no idea how to operate. And so, my partner comes into my family of origin, and my family invariably hurts my partner." Our partners are outsiders to our families. Giles reminds that, "Outsiders are vulnerable. We have to be attentive and protect them and feel comfortable in the group."

One thing is for certain; marriage is a roller coaster, just like life. Often it's really great, and sometimes there are some shitty moments. But nothing is going to be perfect, and why would we want it to be? Growth, especially WITH someone, requires some shit to actually get through. Once you're on the other side, if you're still smiling at your partner, that's what makes it all worth it.

There is no other time in your life when you will receive so much unsolicited advice. Wait, scratch that. This the one of the two times in your life that you will receive an incredible amount of unsolicited advice — the other time being if you decide to have a child. People will start dropping bombs of wisdom on you seconds after asking if you've set a date. And while you don't have to have all the answers up front, you may have to listen to a few tidbits of cringe-worthy anecdotes disguised as advice.

Repeat after us: "People have mostly good intentions." Even though friends, family, and complete strangers may be trying to help you through the process that is getting married, that doesn't mean you have to take any of their advice to heart, if you don't want to. But as editors and writers ourselves, a thoughtful approach here is best. Not everything flung at you advice-wise will be worthy, but there may just be a few pearls of wisdom amongst the deluge. So if something sounds like it might work for you and your partner, try not to brush it off as just unsolicited advice. You may actually be able to use said knowledge to your advantage here. Picking what suits YOU as a couple is what we're all about.

WISHING YOU WELL, YOU ADORABLE LOVEBIRDS!

We're not here to dictate to you how you should plan your wedding. What we have believed since before we put a pen to paper for this book is that couples should yank back control of their weddings, away from the industry and right into their hot hands. We want couples to challenge outdated (and often patriarchal traditions), while walking into this whole thing with an open mind, a ton of creative licence, and some genuine excitement about getting hitched to your person.

Sure, there will be some stress: weddings, like marriage (and life) come with some stresses. Some of its worth sweating. Most of it is not. Our hope is this book has helped guide you toward what is worth stressing over. We hope this made for a wedding with far fewer stresses, fewer tears, less confusion, and more of the good stuff between you and your partner, and also between you and your other loved ones.

Because if you can feel wholeheartedly yourself throughout this process, hopefully this sense of confidence can extend to other areas of your life, as well.

Okay, we'll go now. We don't want to embarrass ourselves or gush more than we should. Enjoy your wedding. Enjoy your partner. And enjoy your marriage.

Xoxo Karen & Michelle

Acknowledgements

Thank you to my partner, Matt, my mom, and my in-laws, Earl and Tia, for all your love and support. Baby girl, you are strong, you are loved, and you can do anything in life that you work hard for. Love, your mama.

Care, I am sorry for that time I made you sit through me telling you how much you mean to me and how much I love you. Kate, my life would just not be the same without you.

To my therapist, Claire. Our weekly chats have grounded me, given me perspective, and have helped me grow beyond what I thought was possible.

To Karen, my co-author and bestie, this book has been a labour of love, blood, sweat, and tears. Thank you for loving me unconditionally through it all. I love you, babe!

— Michelle

Daniel, you not only made space in our lives and our marriage for me to do this, you bigged me up like it was my goddamn birth right to go write this book. I love you beyond words. To my beautiful baby boy and the one in my belly, thanks for the joyful perspective. To my mom for raising me with the word *feminist* as a core part of my identity and vocabulary, and to my brother, who is a masterclass in wit. To Kirstin: I don't know what I did in a past life to meet you in this life.

To Jen McNeely, for giving me my first column and giving so many badass women a platform to find and share their voices at She Does the City. Thank you to the incredible team where I work for giving me the latitude and support to take on this project. Shout-out to Sarah Chamberlin, Deborah Gillis, Lori Spadorcia, and Paris Semansky for modelling what women-helping-women looks like.

And to my co-author, Michelle, for saying yes. I'm grateful with my whole heart for your partnership, talent, and your friendship. I love you, friend.

— Karen

We're immensely grateful for the readers who cared to hear our ideas and for the people that told their stories in these pages, making this book so real.

To our incredible interns from Centennial College's Storyworks program: Alexis Ramlall; Monica Ferguson, Allison Palmer, Monique Thompson, Angelo Cruz, and Marcus Davy (and their indomitable leaders, Mary Vallis and Tim Doyle), we could not have finished this book without you. Go kill out there! To our research assistant, Blythe Hunter, for her tireless work, thank you!

Thank you to our publishing and journalism fairy godmothers: Laura DeCarufel, Robyn Doolittle, Carley Fortune, Marci Ien, Cynthia Loyst, Melissa Leong, Ceri Marsh, and Rani Sheen for showing us the ropes and providing endless guidance, advice, and support.

To Briony Douglas for your generosity and support. Our author shots are exactly what we wanted and beyond. How did you manage that?

To the team at Dundurn, we can't thank you enough for all your support, guidance, and handholding. We're two newbies, who you put a lot of trust in. Scott, Kathryn, Elena, Laura, Heather, and the rest of the team, thank you!

To our editor, Robyn. You took our ideas and made them make sense! Thank you for your patience and your endless phone chats. We appreciate you so much. And to our copy editor, Cheryl, thank you, thank you, thank you!

Kelvin of K2 Literary. Where can we even begin? You took us through *so* many pitches and were always so kind, quick with amazing advice, and, of course, quite a few side-splitting jokes. We love you! Thank you for being the best agent we could ask for.

— Michelle & Karen

Notes

1   Ashley Fetters, "The Pandemic's Long-Lasting Effects on Weddings," *Atlantic*, May 18 2020, theatlantic.com/family/archive/2020/05/coronavirus-could-change-weddings-years-come/611716/.

2   Bella DePaulo, Ph.D., "What Is the Divorce Rate, Really?" *Psychology Today*, psychologytoday.com/ca/blog/living-single/201702/what-is-the-divorce-rate-really.

3   Dr. Chrys Ingraham, in discussion with Karen Cleveland, December 9, 2019.

4   Kirsten [pseud.], in discussion with Karen Cleveland, February 4, 2020.

5   Anu Partanen, *The Nordic Theory of Everything: In Search of a Better Life* (Richmond, UK: Duckworth, 2018).

6   Ellen Lamont, *The Mating Game: How Gender Still Shapes How We Date* (Berkeley: University of California Press, 2020).

7   Natalia Wojcik, "Conflict Diamonds May Not Be on the Radar, but They're Still a Worry for Some," *CNBC*, November 6, 2016, cnbc .com/2016/11/04/conflict-diamonds-may-not-be-on-the-radar-but -theyre-still-a-worry-for-some.html.

8   Wojcik, "Conflict Diamonds."

9   Ann Binlot, "What Makes Lab-Grown Diamonds a More Affordable and Sustainable Alternative to Mined Diamonds?" *Forbes*, December 20, 2019, forbes.com/sites/abinlot/2019/12/20/what-makes-lab-grown -diamonds-a-more-affordable-and-sustainable-alternative-to -mined-diamonds/#4d31c1b64b82.

10   Fotini Iconomopoulos, in discussion with Michelle, May 2020.

11   Allie Jones, "What Changes in the First Year of Marriage?" *New York Times*, July 23, 2020, nytimes.com/2020/07/23/fashion/weddings /what-changes-in-the-first-year-of-marriage.html.

12   "Redditors who have called off an engagement, when did you know it was over and what were the signs that it was time to end things?," Reddit, 2014, reddit.com/r/relationship_advice/comments/1rbn0y /redditors_who_have_called_off_an_engagement_when.

13   Cheryl Strayed, "Dear Sugar, the Rumpus Advice Column #64, Tiny Beautiful Things," Rumpus, February 10, 2011, therumpus .net/2011/02/dear-sugar-the-rumpus-advice-column-64.

14   Joshua T. Pierson, "The Economics of Marriage Contracts," dissertation, George Mason University, 2018, search.proquest.com /openview/dcd52110d44bb24eafa686b7d2525e0b/1.pdf?pq-origsite =gscholar&cbl=18750&diss=y.

15   William Bradford Wilcox, "If You Want a Prenup, You Don't Want Marriage," *New York Times*, April 5, 2013, nytimes .com/roomfordebate/2013/03/21/the-power-of-the-prenup/ if-you-want-a-prenup-you-dont-want-marriage.

16   Wilcox, "If You Want a Prenup."

17   "The Wedding Trend Report 2020," Wedding Academy, January 2 2020, weddingacademyglobal.com/trend-report.

18   Megan Ford, in discussion with Karen Cleveland, January 13, 2020.

19   Crystal, in discussion with Karen Cleveland, November 24, 2019.

20   Tehmina Kazi, "The New Muslim Marriage Contract Should Empower Women," *Guardian*, July 8, 2011, theguardian.com/ commentisfree/belief/2011/jul/08/muslim-marriage-contract-women.

21 Samhita Mukhopadhyay, "Kate Middleton's Wedding Vows: What's in a Word?" *Guardian*, April 29, 2011, theguardian.com/commentisfree/2011/apr/29/kate-middleton-royal-wedding-vows.

22 Laura Hampson, "64% of Weddings Expected to Be Postponed or Cancelled This Year, New Study Shows," *Evening Standard*, April 9, 2020, standard.co.uk/lifestyle/weddings/wedding-industry-coronavirus-statistics-a4410426.html.

23 Pamela N. Danziger, "Will A Booming Economy Bring a Wedding Market Boom? Not Likely," *Forbes*, February 17, 2018, forbes.com/sites/pamdanziger/2018/02/17/will-a-booming-economy-bring-a-wedding-market-boom-not-likely/#6930c45e4270.

24 Tanvi Kumar, "Wedding Services in the U.S.," IBISWorld, December 2018, ibisworld.com/united-states/market-research-reports/wedding-services-industry.

25 Andre Bourque, "Technology Profit and Pivots in the $300 Billion Wedding Space," Huffington Post, December 6, 2017, huffpost.com/entry/technology-profit-and-piv_b_7193112.

26 Stassi Reid, "15 Psychological Tricks to Make Him Propose," The Talko, June 21, 2016, thetalko.com/15-pyschological-tricks-to-make-him-propose.

27 Robert Delahnty, "Will He Ever Marry You?" *Cosmopolitan*, August 17, 2007, cosmopolitan.com/sex-love/advice/a1893/will-he-ever-marry.

28 Jeff Wilser, "5 Ways to Get Your Partner to Propose," The Knot, theknot.com/content/7-ways-to-get-him-to-propose.

29 Renee Wade, "How to Get Him to Propose," The Feminine Woman, undated, thefemininewoman.com/get-him-to-propose/.

30 Josh Spiegel, in discussion with Karen Cleveland, February 12, 2020.

31 Joan DiFuria, in discussion with Karen Cleveland, December 12, 2019.

32 Jim Cutter, *A Groom's Guide to Surviving a Wedding: One Groom's True Story* (self-pub.: AuthorHouse, 2004).

33 Stephen Giles, in discussion with Karen Cleveland, November 28, 2019.

34 Hunter Stuart, "A Message From a Man to Men About Wedding Planning," *Huffington Post*, September 11, 2014, huffpost.com/entry/a-message-from-a-man-to-men_b_5715733.

35 Emily Fitzgibbons Shafer, "Hillary Rodham Versus Hillary Clinton: Consequences of Surname Choice in Marriage," *Gender Issues* 34 (January 4, 2017): 316–32.

36 Stephanie Coontz, *Marriage, a History: How Love Conquered Marriage* (London: Penguin Books, 2016).

37 Suzannah Weiss, "The Sexist Undertones of Wedding Marketing," *New York Times*, October 5, 2019, nytimes.com/2019/10/05/fashion/weddings/the-sexist-undertones-of-wedding-marketing.html.

38 Weiss, "The Sexist Undertones of Wedding Marketing."

39 Dr. Chrys Ingraham, in discussion with Karen Cleveland, December 9, 2019.

40 Becky Pemberton, "Put a Ring on It," *Sun* (U.K.), February 20, 2018, thesun.co.uk/fabulous/5625546/brides-speeches-weddings-wedding-day-traditions-revealed.

41 Matthew Smith, "The Majority of Wedding Traditions Are Still Popular, But Don't Ask the Bride's Family to Pay," *YouGov*, August 10, 2016, yougov.co.uk/topics/lifestyle/articles-reports/2016/08/10/majority-wedding-traditions-are-still-popular-dont.

42 Dr. Andrea O'Reilly, in discussion with Karen Cleveland, August 15, 2017.

43 Julie Miller, "How 20-Year-Old Queen Victoria Forever Changed Wedding Fashion," *Vanity Fair*, April 3, 2018, vanityfair.com/style/2018/04/queenvictoria-royal-wedding.

44 Alex Ballingall, "Liquidator Hopes for a Bridal Wave with Wedding Gown Clearance Sale," *Toronto Star*, November 11, 2014.

45 Morgan McFall-Johnsen, "The Fashion Industry Emits More Carbon Than International Flights and Maritime Shipping Combined. Here Are the Biggest Ways It Impacts the Planet," *Business Insider*, October 21, 2019, businessinsider.com/fast-fashion-environmental-impact-pollution-emissions-waste-water-2019-10.

46 Harvey James, in discussion with Karen Cleveland, May 21, 2020.

47 Karen Klaiber Hersch, "Introduction to the Roma Wedding: Two Case Studies," *Classical Journal* 109, no. 2 (January 2014): 225.

48 Liz Susong, "Everything You Need to Know About the Wedding Veil Tradition," Brides, updated on May 12, 2020, brides.com/story/wedding-traditions-debunked-the-veil.

49 Jaimie Mackey, "Everything You Need to Know About the Bridal Bouquet," *Brides*, July 9 2020, brides.com/story/wedding-bouquet-etiquette.

50   Julie Sprankles, "Ever Wondered Why Brides Carry Bouquets?" *Bustle*,
     July 1, 2016, bustle.com/articles/170372-why-do-brides-carry-bouquets-
     at-weddings-the-tradition-isnt-as-romantic-as-you-might-imagine.

51   KM, "Tiny Stephanotis Flower, Big Impact: Featuring Stephanotis at
     Your Wedding," *Business Weddings*, April 22, 2020, businessweddings
     .com/2020/04/22/stephanotis-flower.

52   "Our Official Guide to the Symbolic Meaning of Wedding Flowers,"
     The Knot, theknot.com/content/symbolic-wedding-flower
     -meanings.

53   Julianne Smith and Liz Susong, "Everything You Need to Know
     About the Wedding Garter Tradition," Brides, Updated on April 10,
     2020, brides.com/story/dispatches-from-a-feminist-bride-part-one
     -garter-bouquet-toss.

54   Caroline Kitchener, "The Bridesmaids Are Multiplying," *Atlantic*,
     November 9, 2018, theatlantic.com/family/archive/2018/11
     /american-weddings-bridesmaids/575404/.

55   Kate Horowitz, "Why Do Bridesmaids Traditionally Wear the Same
     Dress?" *Mental Floss*, February 5, 2016, mentalfloss.com/article
     /74033/why-do-bridesmaids-traditionally-wear-same-dress.

56   Brandon Specktor, "The Weird Reason Bridesmaids All Wear the
     Same Color at Weddings," *Reader's Digest*, rd.com/culture/history
     -of-bridesmaids-weddings/.

57   Sara [pseud.], in discussion with Karen Cleveland, April 10, 2020.

58   Lisi Korn, "Wedding Day 101: Getting in Shape," Forever Events, May
     9, 2016, forever-events.com/getting-in-shape-for-your-wedding-day.

59   Susan S. Lang, "The Bride Wore White and, Maybe, Less Weight —
     But Study Shows She May Have Gone to Extremes for that Svelte
     Look," *Cornell Chronicle*, January 23, 2008, news.cornell.edu/stories
     /2008/01/wedding-day-weight-wishes-lose-more-20-pounds.

60   Ivanka Prichard and Marika Tiggemann, "Appearance Investment in
     Australian Brides-to-Be," *Body Image* 8, no. 3 (June 2011): 282–86.

61   Ivanka Prichard and Marika Tiggemann, "Wedding-Related Weight
     Change: The Ups and Downs of Love," *Body Image* 11, no. 2 (March
     2014): 179–82.

62   Interview with Karen Cleveland, November 3, 2019. The name of the
     interviewee is withheld by mutual agreement.

63 Dr. Sara Santarossa, in discussion with Karen Cleveland, April 10, 2020.

64 Ivanka Prichard and Marika Tiggemann, "Unveiled: Pre-Wedding Weight Concerns and Health and Beauty Plans of Australian Brides," *Journal of Health Psychology* 14, no. 7 (September 2009): 1027-35.

65 Amira Adawe and Charles Oberg, "Skin-Lightening Practices and Mercury Exposure in the Somali Community," *Minn Med* 96, no. 7 (July 2013): 48-9.

66 Fatima Lodhi, in discussion with Karen Cleveland, May 5, 2020.

67 Kate Bratskeir, "Men Describe the Trials and Tribulations of #SheddingForTheWedding," Mic, June 28, 2016, mic.com/articles /144564/mens-wedding-diet-grooms-shedding-for-the-wedding.

68 Theresa E. DiDonato, "Are You Feeling the Pressure for Wedding Weight Loss?" *Psychology Today*, May 30, 2014, psychologytoday.com /ca/blog/meet-catch-and-keep/201405/are-you-feeling-the-pressure -wedding-weight-loss.

69 Amanda Keegan, Kevin Dolak, Yunji De Nies, "The K-E Diet: Brides-to-Be Using Feeding Tubes to Rapidly Shed Pounds," ABC News, April 16, 2012, abcnews.go.com/Health/diet-brides-feeding-tubes -rapidly-shed-pounds/story?id=16146271.

70 Bailey Parnell, in discussion with Karen Cleveland, May 4, 2020.

71 Elaine Lui, in discussion with Michelle Bilodeau, April 2020.

72 Josh Spiegel, in discussion with Karen Cleveland, February 12, 2020.

73 "Feeling the Pressure to be the 'Beautiful Bride.' Anyone Else?" WeddingBee, boards.weddingbee.com/topic/feeling-the-pressure -to-be-the-beautiful-bride-anyone-else.

74 "Teeth on Your Wedding Day — HELP," WeddingBee, boards .weddingbee.com/topic/teeth-on-your-wedding-day-help/.

75 "Teeth on Your Wedding Day — HELP."

76 Ella [pseud.], in discussion with Karen Cleveland, November 5, 2019.

77 Ivy Manners, "Getting Married? Get Strong," *New York Times*, August 8, 2019, nytimes.com/2019/08/08/fashion/weddings/the-perfect-workout-for-your-wedding-dress-silhouette.html.

78 Roy Greenslade, "Gender Stereotyping and Advertising," Independent Press Standards Organisation, July 24, 2017, ipso.co.uk/news-press -releases/blog/gender-stereotyping-and-advertising.

79   "Yes! Husbands stay lovers ... when wives guard against dry, lifeless
      'middle-age' skin!" Palmolive advertisement published in 1938.

80   "Successful marriages start in the kitchen!" Agee Pyrex advertisement
      from Crown Crystal Glass Company Limited, published in *Australian
      Women's Weekly*, January 11, 1947.

81   Jen O'Brien, "Wedding Trends in Canada 2015," *Weddingbells*, May
      11, 2015, weddingbells.ca/planning/wedding-trends-in-canada-2015.

82   Josh Spiegel, in discussion with Karen Cleveland, February 12, 2020.

83   "Magic Kingdom Park Evening," Disney's Fairy Tale Weddings and
      Honeymoons, disneyweddings.com/florida/venues/after-hours
      -experience-magic-kingdom.

84   Megan McDonough, "What's It Like Getting Married at Disney? It's
      Not Always a Fairy Tale," *Washington Post*, May 5, 2017,
      washingtonpost.com/entertainment/whats-it-like-getting-married
      -at-disney-its-not-always-a-fairy-tale/2017/05/04/59390a66-2c24-11e7
      -be51-b3fc6ff7faee_story.html.

85   Kate Lynn Nemett, "The Shocking Truth About Getting Engaged,"
      Zola, December 11, 2018, zola.com/blog/wedding-planning/
      the-truth-about-getting-engaged.

86   Megan Ford, in discussion with Karen Cleveland, January 13, 2020.

87   David Wilkinson and Scott Finkbeiner, "Divorce Statistics: Over 115
      Studies, Facts and Rates for 2018," wf-lawyers.com/divorce
      -statistics-and-facts.

88   Melissa Leong, in discussion with Karen Cleveland, November 28,
      2019.

89   Ashley LeBaron, Derek R. Lawson, Edward Jeffrey Hill, and Sonya
      Britt-Lutter, "Tightwads and Spenders: Predicting Financial Conflict
      in Couple Relationships," *Journal of Financial Planning* 30 (May
      2017): 36–42.

90   Joan DiFuria, in discussion with Karen Cleveland, December 12,
      2019.

91   Alice [pseud.], in discussion with Karen Cleveland, December 9, 2019.

92   "Weddingwire Newlywed Report 2019," WeddingWire, go.weddingwire
      .com/newlywed-report/2019.

93   Melissa Leong, in discussion with Karen Cleveland, November 28,
      2019.

94 "BMO InvestorLine Study: Canadians Plan to Spend an Average of $15,000 on Their Weddings," BMO, newsroom.bmo.com/2014-04-23 -BMO-InvestorLine-Study-Canadians-Plan-to-Spend-an-Average-of -15-000-on-Their-Weddings.

95 *The Ellen Degeneres Show*, airdate October 23, 2019.

96 Beth Montemurro, *Something Old, Something Bold: Bridal Showers and Bachelorette Parties* (New Jersey: Rutgers University Press, 2006).

97 Carly Gieseler, "Gender-Reveal Parties: Performing Community Identity in Pink and Blue," *Journal of Gender Studies* 6, No. 27, February 9, 2017: 661–71.

98 Sheila [pseud.], in discussion with Karen Cleveland, November 13, 2019.

99 SF [pseud.], in discussion with Karen Cleveland, November 18, 2019.

100 Hannah Esmaili, in discussion with Michelle Bilodeau, March 2020.

101 Nazarene University, "The State of Marriage Counselling [Study]," *MidAmerica*, November 3, 2017, mnu.edu/graduate/blogs-ideas /the-state-of-marriage-counseling-study.

Index

About the Authors

MICHELLE BILODEAU

Michelle Bilodeau is a Toronto-based writer and editor, focusing on lifestyle, beauty, fashion, and cannabis. She has worked in Canadian media for nearly 20 years, with staff positions at *Flare*, *Fashion*, and the *Kit*. She has written for *Hello! Canada*, Refinery29 Canada, CBC, Latitude, the *Toronto Star*, and more. Michelle is also a regular on-air contributor for *The Social*.

A graduate of the print journalism program at Centennial College, Michelle has taught and guest lectured at Centennial College. She is also currently a student of the Ontario Psychotherapy and Counseling Program.

KAREN CLEVELAND

Karen Cleveland is a Toronto-based writer. She has contributed to outlets across North America, focusing on lifestyle content such as travel, fashion, beauty, culture, weddings, and wine. For more than 10 years, Karen wrote an etiquette column, Finishing School, that ran on She Does the City and the *Huffington Post*. More recently, she penned the Manners 2.0 column in the *Toronto Star*. She is regularly called upon to comment in the media, including the *New York Times*, *eTalk*, *ET Canada*, Canadian Press, *Weddingbells* and more.

A graduate of York University, Karen has worked in various sectors in marketing and communications. She is a guest lecturer at Ryerson University and York University.